Our Family Table

Recipes & Food Memories™
from African-American Life Models

by Thelma Williams

foreword by Camille O. Cosby, Ed.D.

Maria Elena Cellino, Editor
Al Jackson, Artist and Illustrator

TRADERY
H·O·U·S·E

Thelma Williams
author
Maria Elena Cellino
editor
Al Jackson
artist and illustrator
Keven Wesley
calligrapher

TRADERY
H·O·U·S·E

*Building Community
through the Meal*

Printed in Mexico
for
The Wimmer Companies, Memphis, Tennessee

Library of Congress Cataloging-in-Publication Data
p.cm.

Trade Edition   ISBN 1-879958-14-7
1. Cookery, American.   2. Afro-Americans--Social life and customs.
3. Celebrities--United States--Anecdotes.
1932-
TX715.0916   1993   92-61576
641.59 296073--dc20   CIP

For additional copies, call:
THE WIMMER COMPANIES
1-800-727-1034

DEDICATION

In loving memory of my parents, Anne Emelina and George Benjamin Blaize, who taught me to explore the temptation of wonder.

About the Cover

The quilt, reproduced on the cover, was made by Willia Ette Graham, a third generation quilter. It was given to me as a gift after we met on ABC's Home-Show in February, 1988. Mrs. Graham, now an Octogenarian, was taught the art of quilting by her great-grandmother who was a slave. She resides in Oakland, California and her quilts have been exhibited all over the country, most recently in Hawaii's National Museum. The intricate abstract designs so vividly depicted are from the African influence and heritage handed down through the generations.

TABLE OF CONTENTS

FOREWORD

The human beings, who are portrayed in *Our Family Table*, had to overcome various obstacles to achieve their respective goals. For example, when Charlayne Hunter-Gault desegregated the University of Georgia in Athens in 1961, her life was threatened continuously. However, throughout that horrible period, she was solidly self-disciplined and self-determined. With the support of her family, she prevailed and graduated with a degree in journalism.

Moreover, Dr. Alvin F. Poussaint was one of eight children; his family's economical picture was bleak. Despite the family's low income position, Dr. Poussaint's family encouraged him to earn undergraduate and graduate degrees. Now, he is a psychiatrist. I suspect that these successful people often sat around their respective family tables hearing conversations of love, caring, support and educational goals.

It is time for America's educational institutions — private, public and parochial, to deal with an obstacle far too many Americans face in their daily lives. They need to acknowledge, respect and honor students' learning differences and patterns. Ever since the Ethiopians and the Egyptians created the written word before the birth of Christ[1], millions of people have struggled with reading. Not because the students were unintelligent, but, more than likely, the teaching techniques were not conducive to the students' individualistic learning characteristics.

All human beings have the ability to read. If someone's barrier to securing a career goal is the inability to read, be heartened. You can. Thelma Williams, the author of *Our Family Table*, implemented one teaching/learning technique that anyone can do.

Thelma Williams earned a degree in sociology, taught elementary school for eight years and adult education for another two years, and owned a catering business for twenty years. On numerous occasions, Ms. Williams invited local children to her catering plant: children who had reading deficiencies and didn't know how to perform common tasks, such as, answering a telephone. Ms. Williams felt that she could use her commercial kitchen as a practicum; a place where children could learn to read recipes, weigh and measure foods, write and discuss any details relative to food and preparation. In other words, the children learned basic reading, mathematics, writing and speech skills in her kitchen! Consequently, Ms. Williams successfully meshed education with business.

Every person's kitchen can be a practicum for learning essential educational

---

[1] Edmond, L. and Sweeting, E. (1989), <u>African History</u>. London: Islington

skills. Also, the kitchen is where one prepares food that will nourish the human body. It can be a room where fathers, mothers and guardians can have quality time with their children. After the food has been prepared and set on the family table, it can be a place for exchanging and verbalizing feelings and thoughts and discussing family issues. Thus, the kitchen and the family table become instruments for family bonding.

It is possible that children will learn readily in a kitchen because it is a hands-on environment. Parents or guardians who elicit the help of their children in the kitchen provide them the opportunity to learn and practice these educational skills. Additionally, the kitchen is a place where children can feel wanted, loved and be well-fed. Likewise, if a parent is illiterate, he/she can, with the children, visit the kitchen of a family member or friend who is literate. Hence, the kitchen becomes a communal classroom.

Furthermore, teachers can create kitchen and family table environments in corners of their classrooms. I remember my daughter's teacher doing just that. The teacher used kitchen utensils and food as visual aids for reading, writing and science.

Our Family Table is an important historical book relative to its featured biographies of people who have been victorious. As well, ***Our Family Table*** is important because it can be used in home and classroom kitchens for family fun, togetherness, good food and learning fundamental educational skills.

Camille O. Cosby, Ed.D.
August, 1992

Several generations of our extended family came together at our family table at Easter. As we began to reminisce I felt myself watching the children as they explored with us the exquisite tapestry of our shared past. The table, a place where traditions and core values are passed on, was covered with a lovingly pieced patchwork quilt. As if suspended over that gathering, I glimpsed a vision of what it means to be a family. Children, adults, cousins, mothers, fathers, and brothers, each person seated there like each piece of fabric on the quilt before us, was unique in their own way, occupying their own special place on a mosaic, held in place by threads of love. It came to me that each member of the family is equally important to the beauty and strength of a family just as each piece of the quilt is crucial to its overall beauty. The richly patterned design that twisted, turned and intertwined before us was made beautiful and useful because of a tradition called quilting passed on from one generation to another. In the same way, our lives are made beautiful because others have come before us and shared their special insights and values which we pass from one generation to another in both word and deed. I saw our family members like each square of fabric, connected and strengthened by the threads of our heritage; tradition, a sense of community, insights and values that we seek to pass on over a shared meal. It was then that I understood why my father was so diligent in passing along his values to us. And as we broke bread together, his words came back to me, "Adore words... Cherish knowledge... Practice forgiveness... Look to those who come behind you." That was the fabric of my life.

As I looked at the faces of family members assembled there, each on their own journey, I remembered the risks my parents and others who came as immigrants from that poor island nation of Carriacou had taken. Shared experiences were what had brought family members to where they were today. It was as if I was a little girl again, seated at the family table where my father presided, except now it was me speaking his words....

Adore words... I began... Cherish knowledge. That was a litany my father often repeated. He always had a book or a newspaper and he was obsessed with reading because he was denied an education and became self-taught. At the age of 12, his father died and he had to abandon any thought of additional schooling. To help the family he took on adult responsibilities and went to work. At our family table my father would cleverly throw out some piece of information, whetting our appetite about some new political figure or far-away place and when we asked questions he would say, "You know, this would be a good time for you to go and fill your mind with information about it." Of course we were well versed in the use of the library because my father thought it was the biggest gift you could have. "When you walk to that library the pathway to the world is open to you," he'd say. Then each child was expected to take the next younger child and pass on the tradition.

Practice forgiveness... My father, though a strict and firm disciplinarian, had a great capacity for compassion and forgiveness. My younger sister was disfigured by Hurler-Sheie Syndrome and I helped to care for her, making certain she got her medication and taking her outdoors for a bit of sun. She had an enlarged head and very small body. I remember the sadness and suffering we experienced when she was excluded or ridiculed or stared at. "Practice forgiveness," my father told us, "and look for the larger meaning of life. There are many good people in this world, you will be hurt more severely by these injustices if you are unable or unwilling to forgive."

Look to those who come behind... We called our house the Port of Embarkation and our mother the Sea of Love. We had a constant stream of relatives immigrating to the United States coming to live with us. We always had room to break bread, time to take new cousins to register for school and aunts and uncles to the employment and social security offices. Older brothers and sisters were responsible first for all these new family members. When they went to college or work, it fell to the younger ones. Of course both my father and my mother lived what they talked about. As hurricane season came each year for the islands, out came the barrels. We filled them to the top with clothing and food. When I held back a cherished red dress that was many sizes too small for me, my father reminded me, "A tightened fist makes giving unthinkable and receiving impossible." We learned to gain goodness in life is to give away a lot.

For me, the only way to continue family traditions and values is to model it ourselves. As we finished the meal, talk turned to school, and a cousin offered to help another cousin with his math. Another, fresh out of college, shared insights on courses with a younger family member. It's a continuum, I thought. The progress of the quilt is the progress of life... all the diversionary paths are okay. First our parents are our teachers and life models, but it doesn't stop there. We find our life models in our schools, our neighborhoods, our communities and in the world at large. Each individual has wisdom to share — we have only to look. It is my hope that this glimpse of the childhood families of the life models presented here will create an atmosphere of renewed curiosity about what is possible and warmth for humanity.

Thelma Williams
January, 1993

ACKNOWLEDGMENTS

I offer my sincerest thank you to the twenty-eight life models who allowed me to enter and share those precious memories of their childhood and without whose willing participation this book would not have been possible.

It is with a deep sense of gratitude and profound respect that I acknowledge Dr. Camille Cosby whose constancy of interest, encouragement and magnificent support have been evidenced throughout this adventure. As an educator, children's advocate and humanitarian, her input has been invaluable.

A special mention of appreciation and respect to the following doctors, educators, health care professionals, spiritual mentor and associates who provided me with valued help and guidance whenever it was needed; my late sister, Dr. Rose Blaize Pinckney, Dr. David Viscott, Dr. Mavis Thompson, Mrs. Barbara Smith, Mrs. Delores Snell, Mrs. Carolyn Oliver, Dr. Charles Drake, Ms. Mary Bergerson, Ms. Roberta Benjamin, Ms. Michelle Heron, Rev. Lorentho Wooden, and Judith Griffith Ransom.

Thank you to our two daughters, Keven and Adrienne, for your loving participation and to countless friends and relatives who wanted no thanks, but to be only as supportive and helpful as possible; Daniel Blaize, Mozelle Vample, Marcia Callender, Bunny Lee, Lyle Marshall, Mabel Snowden, Jason Reid, David Daniel, Marc Pinckney, and William Snell. And especially to our dear friend, Rocco Cellino whose courage and strength was an inspiration to me and to all who knew him.

And finally, a huge and special thank you to my wonderful husband, Wesley, whose love and constant encouragement sustained me throughout this remarkable journey.

Publisher's Note:
Thelma Williams is an educator, business woman, activist, who has found life models in all walks of life. A portion of the proceeds of *Our Family Table* will help fund "Our Daily Bread and Cobbler Shop" a retail bakery and youth intervention training center in Atlanta, Georgia that the author and her husband, Wesley Williams will open this year. The center targets youths at risk of dropping out of traditional high schools and provides practical work/life skills through its shop which is open to the general public.

KITCHEN SAFETY AND PREPARATION RULES

1. Wash hands before handling food.

2. Thoroughly wash all fruits and vegetables to remove dirt and insecticides.

3. Read recipe carefully to make sure you have all the ingredients.

4. Set out all ingredients and utensils before you begin.

5. Use cutting board when cutting fruits and vegetables. Always cut in a direction away from you and your fingers. Dice, chop and shred recipe ingredients first.

6. Always use potholders to pick up hot pots or take pans from the oven.

7. Avoid cuts and accidents by washing and storing knives separately from other utensils.

8. Keep dish towels, potholders, aprons, loose clothing, hair, ribbons, and dangling jewelry away from stove burners.

9. Turn pot handles away from stove front.

10. Use electric appliances including blenders, food processors, mixers, can openers and microwaves, etc., only with adult supervision or permission.

Author's Note:

A note about margarines and fats: recently it has been determined that of all the cooking oils canola oil has the lowest saturated fat content. We recommend its use. If canola is not available you may substitute safflower, soy, corn or other vegetable oils with the exception of coconut and palm oil which are highly saturated. Where a specific margarine or oil is suggested in the recipe, such as olive oil, substitutions are not recommended as their use imparts a special flavor.

About the recipes: the recipes contained in *Our Family Table* are nutritional renditions of the recipes given by the models. Because of the serious health problems that are associated with the use of fats and salts in traditional foods, a lighter, healthier recipe is presented here.

Above all this is a book that embarks on a fun-filled trip with the reader to learn how to eat well nutritionally, how to read, how to compute, how to ruminate and enjoy.

ArthurAshe

*It's important for families to pass their values on to
their children. I was always sure of what my
father's values were because he lived them. He
made sure my brother and I knew he expected us to
be home if we didn't have any place special to be.
Home is where he was when he didn't have any
place special to be and that left a lifelong
impression on me when I was growing up.*

Much of what I believe in and the direction my life took is a result of my childhood. When I was very young I had a lot of different childhood illnesses, but even though I was a skinny little kid I bounced back. My dad was always busy teaching my brother Johnny and me how to do things and I didn't want to miss any of the activities.

When I was four years old the city of Richmond hired my father to run Brook Field Playground. My mother, brother, dad and I moved into a house right in the middle of the park that was close to the tennis courts. My mom read to me often and soon I began to pick out words on the page. I was curious about what life was like outside our little part of the world. Reading helped me to discover the interesting world we live in. My dad wanted me to be an excellent reader because he had a sixth grade education and could just get by with his reading and writing. He also insisted that I do my chores on time. I was expected to make my bed, feed the dogs, chop wood and get my studies done.

ARTHUR
ASHE
Athlete/Athletic Consultant
New York, New York

Some of my happiest days were fishing with my father at Yorktown. If we were lucky, we'd catch a few fish. When we arrived home with our catch my stepmother would prepare her delicious spoonbread. Our dad took my brother and me almost everywhere with him and we learned how to hunt, fish, paint and work with tools. He patiently explained how things worked and we learned to be self-sufficient. One August we cut firewood because he knew it was available then and might not be in the winter.

I also found my own way of earning extra money by selling bottles and newspapers. That is how I discovered *National Geographic*, a magazine that tells about the most wonderful places in the world. I got hooked on becoming something special in tennis so I could see the world too.

I was too small for most sports so you can imagine how excited I was when a young tennis player asked me if I'd like to learn how to play. It wasn't easy, but I kept at it. Three years later a coach saw me hitting the ball and invited me to spend time with his other players for coaching and competition. I began to travel to places I'd seen in *National Geographic*.

School was important too because so few people can become professional athletes and earn a living. I also re-examined the feeling my friends and I had that certain jobs were off limits because we were black. In college I studied

Champion Spoonbread

Preheat oven to 400°.

1	egg (separated)	1½	cups water
1	cup non-fat or skim milk	1	cup cornmeal
*1	tablespoon vegetable margarine (melted)	1	teaspoon salt
2	teaspoons baking powder	2	egg whites

You will need

1	helpful adult assistant		measuring cups and spoons
1	1½-quart saucepan	1	1½-quart casserole dish
1	long handled wooden spoon		rubber spatula
1	egg beater		non-stick vegetable spray
1	large and 2 small bowls		

1. Separate egg and place yolk in one bowl, egg white in the second bowl.
2. Add milk, melted margarine and baking powder to yolk and stir until well mixed.
3. Place water in saucepan, add cornmeal and salt and cook over medium low heat for 5 minutes, stirring constantly to thicken and prevent lumps.
4. Add egg yolk mixture to cornmeal mixture. Remove from heat. Pour into large bowl and continue to stir until well mixed.
5. Add the 2 egg whites to egg white in bowl and beat with egg beater until stiff.
6. Fold in stiffly beaten egg whites with rubber spatula into cornmeal mixture then pour into casserole dish which has been greased with non-stick spray.
7. Bake for approximately 40 minutes or until spoonbread puffs up in the center. Serve immediately. The uniqueness of this bread is its pudding-like consistency.

*See margarine note, page 10.

4 to 6 servings

Arthur Ashe

business so I'd have many different career choices when I finished playing tennis. Although I did go on to win the biggest tennis competitions in the world, Wimbledon, Davis Cup, and the United States Open, eventually I retired. My degree in business administration was very helpful as I became an athletic consultant. It also helped when I became National Campaign Chairman for the American Heart Association. Having an education allows you to be the best you can be, in work and volunteer activities.

Roslyn Bell

For me, there are four ingredients in the recipe for a successful life and career. Education, because you can never learn too much. Confidence, because it says "you can!" Creativity, because it separates you from the rest in a unique way. Love, because a genuine love in your heart for doing what you choose to do keeps you alive!

I'm the youngest of six children and was raised in Los Angeles, California. No matter what time of year my mother and father made sure that there were always activities, family dinners and fun projects we could participate in. How blessed I feel to be part of such a large and loving family where I was encouraged to use my God-given talent of creativity.

That creativity was often reinforced on weekend trips to Miss Clinette's Catering Shop when I was a young girl. I decorated the tops of deviled eggs and other hors d'oeuvres to pass the time until my mother finished her work. I'd imagine that I was my mom, making fancy dishes and running a big kitchen.

My mom, Edith Bell, has always been a strong role model. She told me, "Be different, you can do whatever you set your mind and heart to doing," then guided me in doing my best. I remember my first speech tournament in fourth grade was a real highlight. My courage came after watching others successfully compete in something I thought I could do equally as well. I chose the humorous category with the added chal-

ROSLYN BELL

Grand Diplome - Cordon Bleu Chef, Ritz Carlton Hotel Marina Del Rey, California

lenge of making people laugh. I practiced with my instructor, then presented it to my mother. She didn't laugh once! She helped me to improve on my speech by being honest and giving me some pointers. She suggested I be more expressive with facial gestures and to envision myself as the character in the speech. I did more than read a speech the next morning. I really got into the character. The results? I won first place!

I come from a long line of chefs; my maternal grandfather was a chef in New Orleans, my paternal grandmother was a great cook in her own right, and my mother is a chef to the stars of the film industry. I was sixteen years old when I first began cooking professionally. I worked for a catering company and a few restaurants. After college I attended the Cordon Bleu Culinary School in Paris, France. I'd always dreamed of being an actress when I was little. But the excitement and creativity of studying the culinary arts in Paris was drama enough for me. There is no better feeling than the challenge of preparing a dessert. For me, it's a true test of my abilities. And the best satisfaction is when someone doesn't simply like it, but that they love it!

The best and most special skill you need to become a pastry chef is my

Mango Crab Cakes

1 medium mango (peeled and diced)	¼ red bell pepper (diced)
1 large egg	¼ teaspoon white pepper
8 ounces crab meat or imitation crab meat	1 teaspoon Dijon mustard
2 teaspoons fresh parsley (chopped)	½ cup fresh bread crumbs (extra if needed, to bind)
¼ cup green onions (sliced)	2 tablespoons olive oil
	salt (optional)

You Will Need

1 grownup seafood lover	1 medium mixing bowl
1 blender or food processor	1 knife
1 large non-stick skillet	pot holder
large mixing spoon	1 scoop
1 spatula	

1. Place diced mango and egg into blender or processor and purée (about 30 seconds), then pour purée into mixing bowl.
2. In the same blender chop crab meat just until shredded, remove and add to mango mix.
3. Add parsley, green onions, bell pepper, white pepper, Dijon mustard and enough bread crumbs to hold mixture together.
4. Heat olive oil in skillet, and with scoop, form ten crab cakes and place in skillet.
5. Flatten each crab cake with spatula to form fritter.
6. Fry on each side until golden brown.
7. Serve hot.

Yields 10

Roslyn Bell

favorite — it's loving to eat. It's a special sort of eating because you have to train your palate to taste what is too sweet, too bitter, or too dry. Math and chemistry also help because the art of baking requires accurate and precise measurements of ingredients. Understanding how ingredients react chemically to one another determines the end result.

Besides pastry, another of my favorites is seafood. I'm happy to share with you my recipe for Mango Crab Cakes.

Ed Bradley

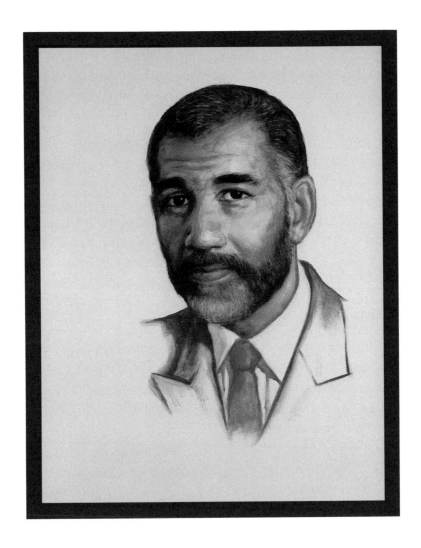

A teacher early on told me, "You can be whatever you want to be." That was at a time when most doors were closed to people of color. That teacher did not say what I could become was within certain boundaries or on a certain track. "You can be whatever you want to be." I believed that.

The experiences I had as a child, living with my mother during the school year and my father in the summers, shaped me and gave me the understanding and the empathy that I have for people and their problems. My parents divorced when I was quite young and both worked at jobs that required long hours. Being a child in a one-parent family is a stumbling block. A tremendous burden is placed on the child and the parent they live with. As a child it's difficult to understand adults and what they are going through. Traveling back and forth between my parents and staying at home alone while my mother worked made me independent. I learned to depend on myself.

Going to school meant a chance to be with other kids. Since I was an only child, that was important to me. The challenge and competition in the classroom of the Catholic school I attended made school exciting. The encouragement of the sisters, especially Sister Ignacita at Holy Providence

**ED
BRADLEY**

**Broadcast Journalist
New York, New York**

in Cornwell Heights, Pennsylvania, kept me focused on getting a good education. Even though my family was quite poor, they had high goals and ideals for me.

On the weekends I looked forward to big family get togethers — they've always been special times for me. My Cousin Eileen had "Over-Home" dinners when young and old family members came from all over the city to visit and eat together. For me, it meant the kind of interacting that goes on among children, and between children and adults. If I'm home and my mom is at work, there is no one for me to interact with. Sunday, at Cousin Eileen's created a sense of belonging. I have warm memories of those afternoons when the kids got together. Later on everyone would sit down to my Cousin Eileen's baked chicken, string beans, biscuits and rhubarb pie and talk turned to what was happening in our lives.

I dreamed of becoming an engineer but later graduated from Cheyney State College with a degree in education and became a sixth grade teacher. A college friend changed my life when he invited me to stop by the radio station where he worked. He let me announce one minute of the news. That was a turning point in my life. I thought announcing was great and I was so determined to get good that I worked as a news reporter and disc jockey for free, to get the experience. That paid off for me and I wound up with two jobs, teaching in the daytime and working at the station at night as a disc jockey. I read the news and called the play by play for basketball games. I enjoyed athletics, so this was easy and interesting to me.

Parisian Couscous Delight

1	cup fresh mushrooms, sliced	⅔	cup couscous (dried pre-cooked semolina)
1½	teaspoons olive oil		
1	cup water	1	medium tomato (chopped)
1	chicken bouillon cube (crushed)	¼	cup currants
1	teaspoon fresh basil (chopped)	1	tablespoon parsley (chopped)
⅛	teaspoon dried oregano	1	tablespoon lemon juice
	dash of black pepper		salt to taste (optional)

You Will Need

1	adult assistant		measuring spoons
1	medium bowl		measuring cups
1	large mixing spoon	1	knife
1	medium saucepan with cover		

1. Wash, dry and slice mushrooms.
2. Heat oil in saucepan, add mushrooms and cook over low heat until tender.
3. Carefully add water to saucepan, add bouillon cube, basil, oregano and pepper. Bring to boiling and remove from heat.
4. Stir in couscous. Let stand covered for 5 minutes.
5. Stir in tomato, currants, parsley, add lemon juice and serve.

Serves 4

Ed Bradley

The opportunity to move to New York, then on to Paris, France, came along. As a young man working in Paris I didn't have much money. I found a restaurant that served couscous, a Moroccan grain dish. The servings were cheap and filling. If money was lqw a meal of couscous could be so filling that I wouldn't have to eat the next day.

My work has taken me around the world and I have a real taste for French, Oriental and Italian foods. My father owned a neighborhood restaurant in Detroit where I worked and cooked when I was a kid. I love to cook. Sometimes when I cook for friends, I put a pot of stock on the stove the night before, and add chicken or vegetables or whatever the recipe calls for. I'll wake up every couple of hours without an alarm clock, check the stock pot then go back to bed. I could spend an entire day cooking. It's a wonderful way to relax after the pressures of broadcasting.

John Bryant

Anything worth having is worth working for.

I was raised in Compton, California. Since I was eight years old, I dreamed of becoming a powerful person who could make a difference in the world. I wanted to count for something and to be someone who could be counted on.

As early as I can remember, I was filled with the dream of operating my own business. When I was ten I convinced my mother to loan me forty dollars to start my first business venture. It was called "The Neighborhood Candy House" and became a financial success overnight. I realized there was a market for a candy store in my neighborhood when I discovered kids would risk being late to school by walking 15 minutes out of their way to visit the nearest store. I decided to meet their needs closer to home. I felt many different emotions as my mother took me to the wholesale candy distributor to make my first purchase. I was excited, nervous, yet confident because my mother and sister both encouraged me. I appreciated my mother's trust in loaning me money to start my business. It was important to me to pay her back and prove her trust in me was well founded. And, important to prove to myself that I could operate my own business even though I was still in elementary school.

JOHN
BRYANT
Banker, Chairman and CEO, Bryant Group Companies, Inc. Los Angeles, California

My fourth grade teacher was inspiring to me. She always encouraged me and was supportive — but most important, she accepted me as I was. Later on, during junior and senior high school I saw the horrors of crime, drugs, and gang warfare. I made up my mind that I would not let them affect me or my goals for succeeding in life. While I was still a teenager I auditioned for a television show and became a child actor. It was exciting learning my lines and the ins and outs of television, but I also knew I wanted to follow that dream of owning my own business.

As a youngster I believed that anything worth having is worth working for. That belief plus the ability to stick to something, has helped me in my career. Patience is important too. I always look to the future and refuse to be intimidated by obstacles or negativity. Wisdom and the ability to get along with and appreciate others are important to someone in my position but I personally believe in being kind, too. I enjoy the ability to help others financially, and emotionally, especially within my own community.

I love individual sports and enjoyed running as a child. Although I like

Chairman of the Board Pasta

6 ounces pasta (penne or rotelle)
½ pound fresh broccoli
1 tablespoon olive oil
2 tablespoons onions, chopped
2 large cloves garlic, chopped
½ cup water
1 medium tomato, diced

1 chicken bouillon cube, crushed and mixed with 1 cup of water
1 tablespoon fresh parsley, chopped
1 tablespoon fresh basil, chopped
2 tablespoons Parmesan cheese, grated

You Will Need
1 adult assistant
12-inch non-stick skillet (with cover)
knife
measuring cup
measuring spoon

slotted spoon
large spoon
plate
serving bowl
potholder

1. Cook pasta according to package directions, drain and set aside.
2. Wash broccoli, trim stalk, cut and separate flowerettes. Dice stalk into ¼-inch pieces.
3. Warm oil in skillet over low heat.
4. Add onions and garlic and sauté for one minute.
5. Add broccoli and ½ cup of water. Turn heat to medium high, and cook until color turns bright green (about 3 minutes).
6. Remove broccoli flowerettes with slotted spoon and set aside on plate.
7. Add tomato, crushed bouillon cube/water, parsley and basil. Bring to rapid boil and cook for 3 minutes.
8. Add pasta. Cover and cook over medium heat for 3 minutes.
9. Return broccoli to skillet. Cook mixture for 3 minutes longer. Turn off heat.
10. Place pasta in serving bowl, sprinkle with cheese and serve.

Serves 4

John Bryant

competing alone, I enjoy getting together with others, especially on Christmas. It's the holiday I like best. A Christmas dinner with broccoli, croissants, and apple pie with ice cream is great but what I really love is pasta. It's tasty, simple to make, light, and has complex carbohydrates which give you energy.

Nathaniel Bustion, Jr.

We know not our divinity. In our very beings we sense an intangible state of perfection just beyond our grasp, just beyond our consciousness, somewhere deeply rooted in our past. We try to reconfirm and reconstruct within our history the transformations through which we have come.

I was born in the deep south, in Gadsden, Alabama and was one of six children. Being part of a large family is an advantage. It gives you instant friends, playmates and people to share your life with. And, you are never lonesome. We always had a wholesome environment and most everyone in my family was creative — musician, tailor, hair stylist, cook, philosopher.

My mother and grandmother used my artwork, my creations in daily life, as a dinner setting or wall hanging. In fact, drawing pictures is one of my happiest memories of childhood. The other is playing basketball with my friends because we were always completely uninhibited. We'd been through a lot of stuff together and I could share my thoughts with them. I was going to be a basketball player when I grew up. I was tall enough, but my love of art won out.

My life's work of art and sculpture gives me so much joy. Through art I experience a bittersweet transformation as I bring my works to life. I use my art to reflect the tragic experience of humanity, molding clay to take the shape and form of what stirs my heart to tell the beauties and horrors I have known and felt. We all need to experience human respect, compassion, enlightenment and love. Through art I can address what is out of balance in my life as well as the tragic parts of history. It is important to remember that society must respect and acknowledge the importance of the various cultures before we can become a universal culture. My art seeks to assist us in understanding that we are all one…pulling strength from each other.

**NATHANIEL
BUSTION, JR.**
Artist/Sculptor/Teacher
Altadena, California

Artists have a compassionate understanding of their subjects. To begin to prepare for a career in art start to work on creative expressions. Experiment with mediums like clay, paint, wire sculptures, pen and ink, pencil sketches, and papier mache. There are many careers related to art where hard work and enthusiastic determination bring success. The things I've struggled the hardest for are the things that I appreciate most. Speaking to a large crowd was once difficult for me. But I learned that it's easier when you really know your subject and stay focused.

Art is important but so are my hobbies; music and cooking. The smell of whole wheat yeast rolls, piping hot from the oven, is a taste I'll never have enough of. That aroma draws people into the kitchen, especially during

Whole Wheat Treasures

Preheat oven to 350°

Baking time 12 to 15 minutes

1	cup stone ground whole wheat flour (sifted)
2	cups all purpose flour (sifted)
1	tablespoon sugar
½	teaspoon salt
1	packet instant yeast
1	cup non fat milk

*1 tablespoon vegetable margarine

½ cup (or more) flour for kneading

1 egg white + 1 tablespoon water for glaze

vegetable non-stick spray

You Will Need

1 grownup baking buddy
measuring cups
measuring spoons
3-quart mixing bowl
9x12-inch baking pan
small saucepan

large wooden spoon
plastic wrap
pastry brush
oven mitts
sifter

1. Mix first five ingredients in 3-quart bowl (non-metallic).
2. Heat milk and margarine in saucepan until lukewarm.
3. Pour milk mixture into dry ingredients and stir with wooden spoon until well mixed.
4. Turn dough onto floured board and knead for 10 minutes using the extra flour until the dough is no longer sticky and is smooth.
5. Spray bowl with non-stick spray and put dough into bowl.
6. Cover the bowl with plastic wrap and let dough rise until it is double in size (45 to 60 minutes).
7. Spray baking pan with non-stick spray. Punch risen dough down; divide and shape into 16 balls and place on baking pan.
8. Beat 1 egg white and 1 tablespoon water until frothy, brush on top of rolls and let rise an additional 20 minutes. Bake rolls in preheated oven from 12 to 15 minutes.
9. Remove from oven with mitts. Cool, eat and enjoy!

*See note for margarine, page 10.

Makes 16

   Nathaniel Bustion, Jr.

Christmas, the holiday I love the best. Why? Because it is the time when people remember to show and share their love and friendship.

Benjamin S. Carson, Sr.

If we want a life of inner peace and of contentment, we have to work for it. For those who want a better quality of life we can go to someone who has reached the goals we're striving for and ask what brought them to where they are and what held them back. Achievers decide to use their ability and their minds to achieve, they observe, ask questions, and learn from other people's mistakes.

There is a Bible story about a boy named Joseph, who went from a slave to become the Prime Minister of Egypt! He was my personal hero and I knew I could become whatever I wanted to be. I wanted to be a doctor but I've got to admit that I was a nearly illiterate "F" student living in a black inner-city neighborhood. By fifth grade, math was one of my biggest problems because I did not learn my times tables. When my mother saw the F on my report card she insisted I learn those times tables even though I complained and called her the meanest mother in the world.

I was a poor reader too, and so my mother required me and my brother to read two books a week and make out a book report. At first we didn't have any idea about how to select books or check them out. But after a month of visiting the library every week and the librarians helping us, I could find my way around the children's section easily. I read all the animal stories I could find, then chose books on plants, minerals, and rocks. I discovered that I could identify the rocks along the railroad tracks near our house from what I learned in books. At school I identified a stone from a volcano our sci-

BENJAMIN
CARSON, SR., M.D.
**Chief of Pediatric Neurosurgery,
Johns Hopkins Hospital
Baltimore, Maryland**

ence teacher held up that not even the smartest kids could identify. As I used more of the knowledge I learned from books I began to have fun at school.

If there is one activity I would encourage for a successful life it would be to read. Structure and sound life models are important too. Find your models in the library, not on television. Our mother was not content to allow us to just read. She was working many hours to make ends meet and decided it was time for us to do household chores. My brother and I argued about every job so mother suggested we write out our own rules of who was to do what. We made a chart of all the things we'd do: mow, wash dishes, mop floors, fold clothing, and the time we would do each job. We even planned properly balanced meals. One of my favorites is chili. At times neighbors criticized our mother. But I am thankful she never stopped demanding that we do our best. Her job was to prepare us for a good life, and she did.

I went on to Yale University where I had to work hard to achieve my goals, then attended medical school at the University of Michigan. My work as the head of pediatric neurosurgery at Johns Hopkins Hospital is both fulfilling and challenging. Everyone has obstacles regardless of where they were born

Red River Chili

1½	teaspoons olive oil		3	tablespoons tomato paste
1	medium onion (chopped)		½	teaspoon cornstarch
1	clove garlic (minced)		1	tablespoon cumin
1	1-inch strip of bell pepper (diced)		1	tablespoon dark chili powder
½	rib celery (chopped)		½	teaspoon dry oregano
1	pound ground turkey or texturized vegetable protein substitute		¼	teaspoon black pepper
			1	15 ounce can whole tomatoes
			1	28 ounce can pinto beans

You Will Need

A chili loving adult buddy
4 quart sauce pan with cover
large mixing spoon

1 knife
  measuring spoons
  can opener
  fork

1. Heat olive oil, onion and garlic in pot over low heat about 3 minutes.
2. Add bell pepper, celery, and ground turkey and stir until turkey turns light color. Raise heat to medium.
3. Continue stirring; add tomato paste and cornstarch.
4. Add cumin, chili powder, oregano, black pepper.
5. Add canned tomatoes, mashing them with a fork.
6. Add pinto beans, stir thoroughly.
7. Cover and simmer 45 minutes.
8. Add salt and pepper to taste.
9. You may enjoy it now, but it's even better reheated the next day.

Serves 8

Benjamin S. Carson, Sr.

and into what situations. The difference between failure and success is how we relate to obstacles. If we see obstacles as fences, we go up to them and stop. If we see obstacles as hurdles we can soar over them, scoot under them or run around them. The human brain is the most sophisticated brain in the universe. Once programmed to view obstacles as hurdles, the brain will rise to the challenge and find a way to overcome whatever is blocking success.

Sister Mary Alice Chineworth

When one must struggle to achieve goals, character is strengthened. To be successful, one must have reasonable goals lest one despair of ever achieving them. Some spend a lifetime struggling yet never achieving and their lives are marked as failures because goals were unrealistic. Self-knowledge here is important. Anything worth having is worth struggling for.

I grew up in a very loving environment. My parents had love for one another, for their children and for everyone else. They were so honest that we grew up thinking that lying was not only wrong but stupid. They were hard working themselves and kind to their employees. I was an extremely shy child. I never said a word in school except to recite lessons or read. And, I would sit at the table during meals and utter not one word. Sometimes my father would show concern about my shyness and try to tease me into talking.

But being shy didn't stop me from enjoying The Mississippi Valley Fair and Exposition when it came to our town each year. My father joined us after work and we ate the picnic dinner my mother had prepared for us. All the carnival rides and brilliant lights thrilled and charmed me. All four children received the same spending allowance for the day and I spent much of mine on cotton candy. Its "disappearing" quality intrigued me. The rest I spent on rides like the "whip" which threatened to dislocate all my joints. Even though the day was filled with excitement, I fell fast asleep during the car ride home.

SISTER MARY ALICE
CHINEWORTH, Ph.D.
Administrator, The Oblate Sisters of Providence
Baltimore, Maryland

I believe if one has a goal to work toward, there will be meaning in life. I was rather unique since I received my call to religious life at age four and was blessed with parents who understood such a call. Practically everything I did during my growing up years was done with that idea of becoming a nun. I think the strongest basis for any career choice is a strong family background. That is something one cannot control, so the next best thing is to reach out to others in love and caring, steering away from self-centeredness. "It is more blessed to give than to receive" is a good rule to live by.

There is an infinite variety of personalities found in a religious organization such as the Oblate Sisters of Providence who have dedicated their lives to the education and evangelization of African-Americans. Our members come from many countries, cultures and backgrounds, making life both exciting and interesting. "Elocution" or public speaking, was mandatory in school when I attended so I did learn to overcome my shyness, and I learned the art of conversation. For an administrator, an outgoing personality, setting goals, and assigning duties are important. For me, my personal enthusiasm for

Friendship Banana Bread

Preheat oven to 350°.

1½ cups all purpose flour
½ cup whole wheat flour
1½ teaspoons baking powder
½ teaspoon baking soda
2 eggs (well beaten)
¼ cup non-fat milk

*⅓ cup vegetable oil
1 teaspoon vanilla
½ cup sugar
2 large ripe bananas (mashed)
¾ cup walnuts (coarse)
  vegetable non-stick spray

You Will Need

1 grownup baker's helper
2 bowls (1 small, 1 large)
1 fork
1 large mixing spoon
  measuring cups

  measuring spoons
  pot holders
  sifter
1 bread loaf pan, 9x5x3-inch
  (non-stick)

1. Sift dry ingredients (flour, baking powder and baking soda) and set aside.
2. Beat eggs in the large bowl until light and fluffy.
3. Add milk, oil, vanilla and sugar and stir.
4. In small bowl, mash bananas with fork.
5. Add bananas into the large bowl. Add sifted dry ingredients and mix well with spoon. Fold in chopped walnuts.
6. Spray loaf pan with non-stick spray.
7. Pour batter into pan and bake in a preheated 350° oven for 50 to 60 minutes or until done.**
8. Turn off oven. Let bread cool for 10 minutes, then remove from pan. Cool for 30 additional minutes before slicing.

* See margarine note, page 10.
** To test for doneness, insert toothpick or skewer into middle of bread. If stick comes out clean, bread is done.

Makes 8-10 slices

 Sister Mary Alice Chineworth

whatever I do, an inquiring mind and average intelligence have given me a zest for life that has not lessened with the years.

Throughout the years the holiday meal I loved best has been Christmas Eve dinner. Some of my favorite foods were fried oysters, asparagus, potatoes, and especially banana nut bread. Christmas was a very special season for me when I could think about all the wonderful blessings God had given to me in the warmth and care of my family.

Kenneth B. Clark

Helping others is an extremely important way of helping oneself to grow up. Education includes more than reading, writing and math. A very important goal of education is to develop sensitivity to the needs of others. With this sensitivity comes the joy of positive interaction.

I was born in Colon, Panama and grew up with one sister who is three years younger than I. My father worked as a clerk for the government of Panama. Some of my earliest recollections were the wonderful times I spent with my mother and my grandmother. Our family moved to the United States when I was quite young. In a short time I began to learn about new customs, games and foods. I remember my mother and grandmother in the kitchen cooking one of my favorite Caribbean dishes, rice and peas. I could hardly wait to hear those magic words, "Dinner's ready, Kenneth." Sometimes the meal also included side dishes of stewed chicken, fried plantains, guava fruit salad, and hot bread. During dinner, my family would ask me about school. It was a special feeling. My mother and my grandmother were always there for me, and they were lovingly pushing me to succeed in school. Both women were always ready to answer honestly the questions I asked them. They believed in my ability, which helped me to believe in myself. I wanted to be a doctor when I grew up. Their confidence in me helped me to pursue that dream, to go to college, and eventually, to receive my doctorate in social psychology.

KENNETH B.
CLARK, Ph.D.
Social Psychologist
Hastings-on-the Hudson,
New York

Early in junior high school I got a taste for writing. A special English teacher brought a lot of excitement to his subject. He helped me to understand that using language could help me communicate some of my observations about myself, my teachers, and others. He encouraged me to enter an essay contest at school. When I received first prize and a gold essay medal, it was one of the highlights for me at that time. Reading and discussing issues with my mother and with others helped me to make some order and sense out of my life.

Although I earned an essay medal, there were parts of school that were difficult. Because I was younger and smaller than my classmates, they wouldn't let me join in their games. So I went to the library because I couldn't compete athletically. As I grew older, I found games suited to my size. I learned to play handball where my size became an advantage because I was quick on my feet.

In working as a social psychologist, my wife, who was also a psychologist, and I did research together on the self-image of children. We found that many children did not have a positive self-image. Along with a positive self-image one must develop a sense of empathy — of being able to feel and

Island Rice and Peas

1	15 ounce can Pigeon Peas (Gandules)*	¼	teaspoon thyme (crushed)
1	teaspoon olive oil	⅛	teaspoon black pepper
1	medium onion (finely chopped)	1	15 ounce can chicken broth (fat removed)
1	clove garlic (minced)	2	cups long grain rice

You Will Need

1	adult assistant		cutting knife
1	3-quart saucepan with lid	1	long handled spoon
	measuring cup	1	can opener
	measuring spoons		

1. Drain peas and reserve liquid.
2. In saucepan sauté over low heat, onions and garlic in oil until transparent.
3. Add drained peas, thyme, pepper and cook for five minutes.
4. Mix reserved liquid and broth with water to make 4 cups.
5. Add rice to peas and stir to mix well.
6. Add the 4 cups of liquid; stir, raise heat to high and when mixture comes to a boil, lower heat and cover.
7. Cook 25 to 30 minutes until all water is absorbed and rice is tender.

*Note: Pigeon Peas (Gandules) may be purchased in Caribbean or Hispanic markets.

Serves 8

Kenneth B. Clark

identify with the feelings of others. That is important for all of us. There were many frustrations too. It was difficult to accept racial segregation in schools which I felt was very detrimental to children and blocked their positive self-image. Since I enjoyed helping others, I never gave up presenting my ideas and putting them into practice whenever possible. Part of my research and writings, which I conducted in collaboration with my wife, were used in the Supreme Court decision of *Brown vs. the Board of Education of Topeka, Kansas*, which raises questions about segregated schools.

As a social psychologist, I talked and observed people and studied how people related with others. Learning more about my fellow human beings hasn't discouraged me. I am still concerned with advancing the humanity in human beings, and in helping people to understand and accept each other.

Norwood J. Clark, Jr.

*Achieving goals is just like living life.
We have to grow through it and not just go
through it. Achieving a goal only becomes
a struggle when you take your eyes off
the prize. So, if you stay focused, there is
no struggle.*

I was born and raised in a little town near New Orleans, Louisiana. Near my home there was a rice field and a sugar cane field with the mighty Mississippi River out front. About once a month my parents took me to ride "The President", a huge vessel that fascinated me with the way it mastered the river. We'd stroll up and down the riverboat as it made its way down the river but we never stayed aboard overnight nor did we ride at night. It was a mixture of both good and bad times because there were certain restrictions for people of color to abide by.

My parents, aware that racism and prejudice stem from fear and that fear stems from lack of knowledge, never embraced the disease of racism or prejudice in our home. After attending segregated schools and not having any friends of non-color, as fate would have it, my first job out of college I worked at an all white company in San Francisco. That was the rebirth of my confidence in mankind and the American dream. My colleagues treated me with the dignity and respect that all individuals from every walk of life need and deserve. That had always been true of my family where my mother, an educator for 36 years, taught me the value of giving back to those who were in dire need.

NORWOOD JOSEPH
CLARK, JR.
President, Uncle Darrow's Cajun Candy Company

As an only child I had to overcome wanting to always be liked. My peers treated me special in an unspecial way and I became a loner. I learned, out of those negative experiences, not to do things that I didn't feel good about. I have not allowed my peers to put pressure on me, even my adult peers now. Asthma also had a traumatic effect on my life. My activities were limited and so I spent time reading and dreaming of becoming a television producer or owning my own business.

That dream of owning a business came true when I started Uncle Darrow's Cajun Candy Company. Family members always encouraged me to be the best in anything that I attempted to do. They told me that if I had the will and desire, I would never be denied. I can honestly say that it works. If I did go back in time to my childhood I would want to take the knowledge that I can be anything I want to be in this physical life.

As a boy, I remember when the ladies from our church would come over for meetings and my mom made her delicious tea cakes. I can still smell the aroma. Those early memories inspired me to manufacture candies, pastries,

Mrs. Clark's Teacakes

Preheat oven to 350°.
Bake 8 to 10 minutes.

1½ cups flour	1 large egg
1½ teaspoons baking powder	1 teaspoon vanilla
3 extra tablespoons flour	3 tablespoons milk
*¼ cup margarine	vegetable non-stick spray
⅓ to ½ cup sugar	

You Will Need

1 grownup partner		sifter
cookie sheet		oven mitt
measuring spoons		cooling rack
large mixing spoons	1	2-inch biscuit cutter
measuring cup	2	mixing bowls
metal spatula		

1. Sift 1½ cups of flour and baking powder and set aside, dust cutting board with the 3 extra tablespoons of flour.
2. Spray a 12x16-inch cookie sheet with vegetable non-stick spray and dust with flour.
3. Cream the margarine in the mixing bowl until soft, add sugar a little at a time and beat until light and fluffy.
4. In a small bowl beat 1 egg until light, then add it to the sugar-margarine mixture; stir in vanilla.
5. Carefully fold in flour mix (½ cup at a time) with milk (1 tablespoon at a time) until well blended.
6. Spoon the mixture onto the board (mixture will be soft) pat it and spread it gently until it is coated with the flour from the board and is ¼-inch thick.
7. Use the biscuit cutter to cut the teacakes (about 12).
8. Place the teacakes onto the cookie sheet.
9. Place cookie sheet in oven. Bake for 8 to 10 minutes.
10. Use mitts to remove cookie sheet from oven. Use spatula to remove teacakes from cookie sheet.

*See margarine note, page 10.

Makes 12 to 14

Norwood J. Clark, Jr.

and confections. As I spend time in the factory making candy, and enjoying the different backgrounds of all the workers, there is a bond that makes me feel special. That is the part of the job that appeals to the child in me, because all children want to be made to feel special.

Johnnetta B. Cole

While I think struggle can strengthen one's character, there are some things we shouldn't have to struggle against, like racism, sexism, and severe poverty. We should just eliminate them.

I had a wonderful and warm family. My dad was very affectionate and playful with us. My mother was a professional woman who also loved rearranging and decorating our house. She was a no nonsense woman who nevertheless would go into tickling sessions with me and my two siblings. My mom took special care of our family but she always did for others as well. I try to emulate all of my mother's strengths.

Both of my parents worked, and yet we spent a good deal of time together as a family. During my early years my maternal grand aunt, NaNa looked after me, and I remember with great pleasure the wonderful meals she prepared for our family. My big sister and I adored our baby brother. His arrival encouraged me and my sister to turn him into our "patient" as we played doctor and nurse. To anyone who asked "and little girl, what are you going to be when you grow up?" I always said, 'A baby doctor.' My parents and teachers encouraged me to become just that. In college I became fascinated with anthropology. My mom's advice was, "Follow your dreams and whatever you do, do it well!"

JOHNNETTA B.
COLE, Ph.D.
President, Spelman College
Atlanta, Georgia

The biggest stumbling block I had as a child was the intense racism that surrounded me in the Jim Crow south of the 1940's in Jacksonville, Florida. My family and teachers helped me figure out that the problem was not my inferiority. I wasn't inferior. The problem was the belief of white folks that I am less than they. Learning that lesson has stood me in good stead.

I always loved school and I had a special fondness for the public library. I also loved to play all the games like hide 'n seek, jacks, monopoly, hop scotch and jump rope, especially double dutch.

The best preparation for becoming a college president is to nurture a love affair with learning. Develop the habit of going to a library every week, and reading a book for fun before going to bed. For life and career success try large amounts of hard work, organization and discipline, interest in succeeding but also in helping others to succeed, faith in your people and your God, and the willingness to be a friend and receive friendship from others. I gain the most satisfaction and fulfillment from my job when I see the blossoming of a Spelman sister, a young African-American woman who has discovered herself and the world of ideas and is ready to take on all else who will challenge her.

Heavenly Buttermilk Biscuits

Preheat oven to 425°.
Baking time 10 to 12 minutes.

2 cups self rising flour, sifted	1 tablespoon honey
½ tablespoon baking soda	1 cup buttermilk
3 tablespoons unsalted corn oil margarine	1 egg white

You Will Need

an adult biscuit lover helper	rolling pin
measuring spoons	pastry brush
measuring cups	mixing bowl
fork	floured board
sifter	cookie sheet (non-stick)
2-inch biscuit cutter	

1. Sift 2 cups flour and baking soda into mixing bowl.
2. Add margarine using fork, cut into the flour mixture until it looks like coarse meal.
3. Add honey to buttermilk. Using fork, add buttermilk mix to flour mix to make a soft dough easy to roll out.
4. Knead (fold dough over and press lightly with heel of hand) about 8 times on floured board. Remember, too much handling will produce tough biscuits.
5. Roll or pat dough to about ½ inch thickness.
6. Cut dough with biscuit cutter, place on cookie sheet.
7. Beat egg white in cup with fork.
8. Brush top of biscuits with beaten egg white.
9. Bake in 425° degree oven for 10 to 12 minutes.

Makes 12

Johnnetta B. Cole

On the weekends my husband and I like to concoct dishes. Being in our kitchen reminds me of being in the kitchens of my childhood where there was always a good feeling and adults would let you "lick the bowl". I do follow recipes, but always with a dash of my own ideas. I find cooking to be a very creative exercise, and I really like to do it.

There are special break times like Thanksgiving that refresh me. It's a time for family and friends to share the love and friendship of each other and a delicious turkey dinner with all of its trimmings. NaNa's homemade biscuits for breakfast is the way we began Thanksgiving Day and it is a memory that I cherish with delight.

Camille O. Cosby

*I am happy, satisfied and fulfilled when I
know that I have challenged myself and
others to produce works of art that are
truthful, intelligent and respectful of
people's sexes, cultures and religions.
Moreover, those challenges make my job
exciting and interesting.*

I was born in the nation's capital, Washington, D.C., and am the eldest of one sister and two brothers. My parents treated their girl children equally with their boy children. All of us were expected to perform the same household chores because our parents equally shared in their household chores. I was the organizer in my family, although my brothers and sister thought I was just plain bossy.

There was a warm, communal spirit in my family's kitchen. I loved to prepare foods such as fried chicken and lemon meringue pie but I thoroughly disliked cleaning the dishes, pots, pans, stove and sink. Dinner time was a happy time, especially when my grandfather described his first encounter with my grandmother. He was so smitten with her that he accidentally backed into a full clothes line and became entangled in the clothes. Although everyone laughed and laughed at his stories, we also never tired of them because they confirmed the love that existed between my grandparents.

CAMILLE O.
COSBY, Ed.D.
Producer
Santa Monica, California

My grandparents were activists; they never backed away from making a wrong a right. My parents have been lifelong, strong, positive influences in my life. They encouraged each of their children to obtain a college degree and establish career goals. When I was growing up, I dreamed of becoming a high school teacher, and my parents and grandparents inspired and encouraged me. My parents have always been truthful, lovable, sincere and unselfish. I admire the way they have lived their lives and I have tried to emulate their behaviors and values.

There are many parts to life and career success. I believe in love of self and family, unselfishness, tenacity, positive thinking, and a good education. I believe in reciprocal friendships based on trust, honesty and respect, and reciprocal respect and trust between employers and employees. Moreover, I believe that it is important to invest in human beings; that is, to provide educational opportunities for people who cannot afford vocational and college/university tuitions.

My job as a record, video and film producer is a serious responsibility to the performing artists, the listeners/viewers, and myself. Producing appeals to me because it is creative. It is like piecing puzzle parts to form a picture. Long hours filming and editing scenes are all a part of the final product.

Bread Pudding Suprise

Preheat oven to 350°.
Baking time: approximately 45 to 60 minutes.

4	cups of day old French bread (torn into one inch pieces)	1	teaspoon vanilla
2	cups milk	½	teaspoon nutmeg
1	cup apple juice	⅛	teaspoon cinnamon
1	whole egg plus	½	to ¾ cup raisins
4	egg whites	*1	tablespoon margarine
⅓	cup sugar	6	tablespoons fresh bread crumbs
		1	tablespoon brown sugar

You Will Need

	absolutely one adult measuring cup	1	small frying pan
1	2-quart saucepan	1	4x8-inch bread pan
1	2-quart mixing bowl egg beater or whisk measuring spoons	1	large mixing spoon baking pan (larger than bread pan) oven mitts

1. Warm the milk and apple juice in saucepan.
2. Beat egg and egg whites in bowl; add ⅓ cup sugar, vanilla, nutmeg and cinnamon; add bread, warm milk and juice. Let mixture sit 20 minutes.
3. Grease the bread pan with one half of the margarine.
4. Layer the bottom of the pan with ⅓ of the mixture; sprinkle with ½ of the raisins, repeat procedure for next layer, then end with bread mixture on top layer.
5. In frying pan melt remaining margarine; add fresh bread crumbs until golden; add brown sugar, then sprinkle the mixture over layered bread pudding.
6. Place bread pan into larger pan, which contains enough hot water to come half way up the side of the bread pan.
7. Bake until knife inserted into pudding comes out clean. Remove from oven with mitts, cool, then refrigerate.

*See margarine note, page 10.

Serves 12

Camille O. Cosby

Patience and hard work come before great project results.

I love this bread pudding recipe because it makes me feel connected to my grandmother and to my father. My father learned the bread pudding recipe from his mother, then gave it to me and my brothers and sister. It is a recipe that will be passed to my children and, hopefully to their children. Consequently, the bread pudding recipe will be perpetual.

Dorothy Cropper

Very few people win Lotto or become million dollar basketball players. Most people can achieve a comfortable life if they have earned and worked for skills that prepare them for jobs and professions.

Much of my youth was spent as a member of the only black family living in a working class Italian-American neighborhood. For obvious reasons, often I did not have other children with whom to play. It was necessary to entertain myself — to follow pursuits that did not require others. Reading, painting and music became friends that have stayed with me through my life. The ability to enjoy being by myself has been a lifetime benefit to me.

We were the first family in our neighborhood to own a television. My father was ill and my mother thought it was important to have this new entertainment source while he was convalescing. It was so small we called it the postage stamp. We never allowed it to interfere with mealtimes. In the evenings we always ate dinner together — my mother, father, brother and me. We generally had dinner in the kitchen during the week and in the dining room on Sunday. Mealtime was a time for everyone sharing the news of the day, plans for the future, thoughts and ideas. I was not a finicky eater. I liked most of the dishes that Mother made. Among them were curried, sautéed shrimp and oxtail stew. My favorite non-holiday dish was fricassee chicken. It was cooked slowly in a large pot with milk added towards the end with dropped, soft, fluffy dumplings.

DOROTHY CROPPER

Judge, New York State Court of Claims New York, New York

I had chores that I was expected to do, but cooking wasn't one of them. My mother didn't teach me to cook, but I had a few recipes I knew how to make, like custard. She was a constant support and encouraged my skills. My piano lessons and painting lessons, paid for before and after she was widowed, have provided me with great pleasure throughout my adult life. My father died while I was in high school but there was never any thought that my brother and I wouldn't help in the home, study hard and go to college while my mother ran her business.

My mother helped me financially to accomplish my desire to become a lawyer, even though she thought the teaching profession a more ideal one for a woman. My desire to become a lawyer stemmed from my belief that my skills were appropriate to the field and that I could help others through the profession. My work as a judge is interesting and stressful and carries a great amount of responsibility. It's interesting because of the variety of cases and constantly changing persons in the courtroom including lawyers, defendants, jurors and witnesses. It is stressful sometimes because of the nature of our legal process which can, on occasion, become very heated.

Hurry! A Shrimp Curry

1 tablespoon olive oil
½ medium onion, chopped fine
1 large garlic clove, minced
1 teaspoon fresh ginger, minced fine
1 teaspoon fresh parsley, chopped
⅛ teaspoon thyme
1 small tomato, seeded and chopped
2 tablespoons curry powder

¼ teaspoon black pepper
1 tablespoon fresh lime juice
½ tablespoon flour
1½ pounds fresh medium shrimp, shelled and deveined
1 cup canned or homemade chicken broth, fat removed
1 tablespoon mango chutney (optional)

You Will Need
1 adult curry-loving assistant
1 large skillet
measuring spoons
measuring cups
cutting board

cutting knife
can opener
large spoon
potholder

1. Heat oil in skillet and sauté onions until lightly browned.
2. Add garlic, ginger root, parsley and thyme. Cook for 3 minutes longer.
3. Add tomato, curry powder, black pepper, lime juice and stir for 3 minutes over medium-high heat. Heat until well mixed.
4. Sprinkle flour over mixture and stir to mix well.
5. Add raw shrimp, stirring and cook for 2 minutes or just until shrimp start turning pink and begin to curl.
6. Stir in broth and chutney and cook for an additional 3 minutes until shrimp are cooked and sauce is heated throughout and well blended. Serve over hot cooked rice.

Serves 4 to 6

Dorothy Cropper

As a judge, a part of my job requires me to control the legal process, keeping it orderly, fair and dignified. Because my decisions affect people I must carry out my duties responsibly in a thoughtful, careful way. For me, my most important skill is language and the ability to communicate with people of all races and nationalities. Good English is not a racial sellout, it is a necessity for achievement in the marketplace and elsewhere. The message of *Pygmalion* and *My Fair Lady* is still valid.

David N. Dinkins

*Never stop trying. Stay in school,
knowledge is the foundation for a good life.
Learn to read, learn proper manners, learn
to accept and encourage others,
and, learn to accept yourself.*

My family came to the United States from Africa in the hold of a slave ship. My parents were raised, like their ancestors, in the state of Virginia. When they finished school they moved to Trenton, New Jersey.

One of my earliest memories and one of the happiest days of my life was when my little sister, Joyce, was born. When my sister and I were quite young my parents divorced. My mother, sister and I went to live with my grandmother in Harlem, but often we would visit my father, who owned a barber shop. As the older brother, I was put in charge of making decisions for my little sister and we developed a close friendship. Sometimes she tried to get me to allow her special treats or to get out of doing homework, but I tried to think of what was best for her in the long run. My mother and grandmother were often at work, they both worked as housekeepers, so it was up to me to look out for my sister. My mother worked for a judge and earned a dollar a day.

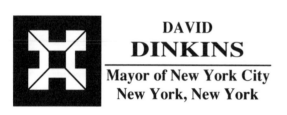

DAVID
DINKINS
Mayor of New York City
New York, New York

As a child, I dreamed of becoming a lawyer when I grew up even though my best subject in school was math. Both my parents made sure my sister and I knew right from wrong, fair from unfair. They expected us to do the right thing. The organization of the law and the belief in justice for everyone no matter what their race or nationality were extremely important ideas to me. I have seen plenty of discrimination in my own life and if I could find a way to help eliminate some of the unfairness in the world, then I wanted to do it.

I loved to spend my youthful hours in the library reading. My stepmother was an English teacher and she encouraged me to discover the world through books. I honestly believe that reading is the most important activity in which a child can engage. I am thankful that my family stayed involved, asking me about the books I was reading and reading to me. There is no limit to what you can become, no matter where you begin, and it can all start with books. I am also fortunate that my high school Latin teacher, Ms. Berniece Munce, was interested in my hopes and plans for the future and helped me to figure out how I was going to achieve them.

While my eye was always on the future, I also liked the present, and especially the holidays such as Christmas when all the members of my family came together. My father was a great chef and his baked oysters were

Zesty Egg White Omelette with Herbs

| 4 | egg whites | 1 | teaspoon soybean oil |
| 1 | tablespoon chopped fresh herbs (a combination of any or all of the following herbs may be used: basil, tarragon, thyme, parsley and chervil) or 1½ teaspoons dried mixed herbs | 1 | tablespoon Parmesan cheese |

You Will Need

1	adult assistant	1	8-inch non-stick skillet
1	bowl		wooden spatula
1	whisk		pot holder
	measuring spoons		

1. Place egg whites in mixing bowl.
2. Whisk egg whites slightly.
3. Add 1 tablespoon of herbs to egg mixture and mix well.
4. Heat frying pan on low heat, add oil to cover surface, and pour in egg mixture.
5. When eggs begin to set, lift edges with spatula and tilt skillet to let uncooked egg run to the bottom. Sprinkle Parmesan cheese over the omelet.
6. Continue cooking omelet over low heat and when it is cooked to an even consistency, fold the omelet over into a half circle and cook until fluffy.

Serves 2

David N. Dinkins

a family favorite. Besides oysters, my favorite foods are chicken, because it's healthy for you, greens, corn bread, peach cobbler, and a tall glass of milk to drink.

For a delicious meal, I'd like to share an omelet recipe with you. It's nutritious, and really easy to prepare.

Charlayne Hunter-Gault

*If we tried to understand the humanity
of each other, a lot of the problems we've
created for ourselves would have never
occurred.*

I can still see my grandmother pulling weeds from the big garden behind our house in Covington, Georgia. She'd plant tomatoes, corn, collards — all kinds of vegetables, but always had plenty of room for her flowers. I share my grandmother's love of flowers just as I share her love of knowledge and learning. She had only a third grade formal education so she educated herself. She was one of the most adventurous, curious, informed and involved people I have ever known. A lot of the activities she was involved in centered around the church.

Sunday dinner was always a big deal in our family. We'd be in church almost all day and I'd always be starving by dinner time. We were regular church goers, always preparing, dressing up. I squirmed a lot as the service grew longer and longer and so I'd usually get a "switching" before dinner.

But my grandmother's Sunday dinner, complete with dessert, always wiped away my tears and any bad memories. I loved being in the kitchen watching my grandmother cook without a recipe or note of any kind. She

CHARLAYNE
HUNTER-GAULT
Journalist
New York, New York

turned out picture perfect dishes every time. My favorite foods were corn, okra and tomatoes, all grown right out in our backyard. Corn, anything cooked with corn in it appeals to me because it reminds me of the tastes of my childhood and possibly the Native American part of my heritage. That's why I like leftover cornbread eaten with buttermilk, a real southern favorite. But the part of the meal I liked best was Ambrosia. We had it on holidays and it's still my all time favorite with oranges, coconut, maraschino cherries and pecans.

I used to dream of becoming a journalist when I grew up. Part of that comes from my grandmother who subscribed to three newspapers and read them from front to back each day. My father was overseas much of the time as a Chaplain in the United States Army so my mother and grandmother raised me. Although grandmother was a personal hero for me, the comic strip character, reporter Brenda Star, was a childhood inspiration. In fact, writing papers and writing for the high school newspaper were the best things about school for me. I was thrilled when I was named the editor of the *Green Light*, our high school paper. It was a chance to spread my wings and try out my own ideas for the school paper. Of course there were deadlines to meet and last minute glitches when the copier didn't work right or someone didn't get

Grandmother's Ambrosia

3 cups pineapple chunks (fresh or canned)
2 bananas, sliced across
4 oranges, peeled, seeded, and sliced

1 cup fresh cherries, pitted, or 1 small jar of maraschino cherries, drained
½ cup pecan halves
1¼ cups grated coconut (fresh or canned)

You Will Need
1 happy adult assistant
1 large serving bowl (non-metallic)

mixing spoon
slicing knife
grater

1. In large bowl, layer ½ of the fruit in the following order: pineapple, bananas, oranges, cherries, and pecans. Sprinkle with ½ the coconut.
2. Repeat procedure for second layer. Use the cherries and pecans to decorate top of the coconut.
3. Serve the Ambrosia at once or refrigerate.

Serves 8

Charlayne Hunter-Gault

their story in on time. But once the work was done, and the papers were sold, it was exciting to watch students reading our paper.

I knew writing would be my life's work. I wanted to get a degree in journalism but the only college in the state of Georgia offering this course of study was the University of Georgia. There were no black students at the college and so one of my classmates, Hamilton Holmes, and I filed a lawsuit to force the school to desegregate. Eventually I became the first black woman to graduate from the University of Georgia. It was a difficult two and a half years but I earned the degree in journalism I wanted. I also learned a lot. I became more sensitive to other people and more interested in them. And, being one of the first two black students at an all-white school opened up a door to black students that had been closed. That was important to me.

I love doing stories about people because I really care about them and their problems. Along with writing short stories I became an investigative reporter after moving to Washington, D.C. Writing has opened up so many opportunities in my life. I've anchored news programs, written my autobiography and worked as a journalist for the Public Broadcasting System, all because I refused to "stay in my place" and give up my dream of attending the school in my home state.

Judith Jamison

*As a child I dreamed of becoming a pilot
when I grew up, then I found there are
many ways to soar. Dance is my way.*

Sports and music and dance kept me happy and healthy when I was a child growing up in Philadelphia, Pennsylvania. My mom had been an athlete and also taught school. My father had once worked as a singer and pianist. I was naturally drawn to musical, rhythmic things and when I started playing the piano, it was my father who gave me lessons. Of course, since he was the teacher, he made sure I got my practice in, and did it right.

I've been dancing since I was six years old. I loved school, the variety of students and the passion of my teachers. I've always enjoyed reading and swimming but dance came first for me. I didn't know it then, but dancing taught me about commitment and discipline. Strangely enough, I didn't realize my life's work was going to be dance even though it has always been magical for me. I did want to be a pilot, but when I graduated from high school I was accepted at Fisk University in Nashville, Tennessee. I decided to study psychology. Psychologists observe people, they are interested in the way people develop, how people get along with each other. Dancing and psychology are somewhat related. Dancers tell a story about people, they share with you a piece of history. After three semesters at Fisk, I knew that I wanted to dance more than I wanted to be a psychologist and so I enrolled in the Philadelphia Dance Academy.

JUDITH
JAMISON
Artistic Director, Alvin Ailey
American Dance Theater
New York, New York

Along with performing modern dance I also wanted to choreograph. Choreographers create dances for dancers to perform. *Cry* is a fifteen minute dance piece created for me by Alvin Ailey. It celebrates the triumph of black women from the time of slavery through today. To create that kind of dance I needed to learn how to teach dance and also be able to understand lighting and costuming. For me, the best way to learn was to continue dancing. I had some inspiring teachers and mentors, Carmen de Lavallade and Alvin Ailey, and I also took special classes in dance history and dance composition.

Dedication, discipline and commitment really pay off when a dancer is on stage and communicating with the audience. Another important aspect of my work is sharing it with the next generation. For me, working with children in our outreach programs, showing them how to move, watching their excitement, and showing them our love of dance, is wonderfully fulfilling.

Premiere Sweet Potato Pie

Preheat oven to 350°.

1	9-inch pie shell (see Broccoli Quiche, page 67, for crust, or purchase refrigerated pie shell)	½	teaspoon cinnamon
		⅓	cup sugar (or ⅓ cup brown sugar, firmly-packed)
1½	pounds sweet potatoes or yams (approximately 3 medium size potatoes)	½	teaspoon nutmeg
		1	cup skimmed evaporated milk
1	egg (or 2 egg whites)	*1	tablespoon margarine, melted
		1½	teaspoons vanilla

You Will Need

1   energetic adult assistant
   knife
   fork
   measuring cups

   measuring spoons
   large mixing bowl and spoon
   pot holder
   electric mixer

1. Wash potatoes and bake in oven until done (45 to 60 minutes).
2. Using potholder, remove from oven, cut potato in half and scrape pulp into bowl of electric mixer.
3. Beat potatoes until smooth.
4. In large mixing bowl, beat egg with fork until frothy. Add potatoes, cinnamon, sugar, nutmeg, milk, melted margarine and vanilla. Stir with large mixing spoon until well mixed and smooth.
5. Pour sweet potato mixture into pie shell. Place on middle oven rack and bake 40 to 50 minutes or until knife inserted in center of pie comes out clean. Remove from oven with pot holders and cool.

*See margarine note, page 10.

Serves 8

Judith Jamison

Knowing my own personal history has been tremendously helpful for my dancing. Family get-togethers have always been important for me and provided that history. Labor Day picnics that included cousins, uncles and aunts were filled with sharing old stories and histories and playing with the other kids. Those occasions created a sense of well-being that didn't go away. Perhaps that is why I always looked forward to Thanksgiving, not only did the larger family gather with young and old generations, but we had my favorite foods. My mother's sweet potato pies were the highlight of the meal, but first we had turkey and dressing, ham and biscuits, corn bread, string beans, and little fruit cups.

Mae C. Jemison

Do your best. Find out about the world and all of its opportunities and you will begin to understand the variety of careers available to you. Don't blindly follow others: read, learn, discover, then make your own choices.

I was born in Decatur, Alabama, but I think of Chicago, Illinois as my hometown. I have a sister and a brother and wonderful parents who have always loved us and helped us to explore the world. When I was in fifth grade my parents began helping me find books on astronomy because of my intense curiosity about space. In fact, I was curious about almost every subject that came along. I could often be found in the school library reading about prehistoric and extinct animals. I wondered about evolution, about anthropology, and of course I was beginning to find the answers in the library.

We had a fun type of family. We'd sit around the table, my parents, brother and sister, an aunt or an uncle or two, and talk about the world, about Africa, about trips we planned to take, and about my personal heroes, people like Julius K. Nyerere, Miriam Makeba, and my teachers Dorothy Miller and John Taylor.

MAE C.
JEMISON, M.D.
Astronaut,
Lyndon B. Johnson Space Center
Houston, Texas

Besides the academic parts of school I loved to dance, which made the pom-pom squad the perfect after school activity for me. I also was a member of the modern dance troupe. That was good experience for me when I went to college and tried out for student productions that required dance. I also found that other hobbies and interests kept life interesting and exciting. I learned about photography, began collecting African art, learned how to ski and sew and took up weight training. To relax I'd make my favorite cracked wheat sandwich and then settle into a good book.

I knew that I wanted to be a doctor, but I also wanted to learn more about my African heritage, so I earned degrees in both science and Afro-American studies while at Stanford University. With that background I completed a medical degree at Cornell University. After completing my internship at Los Angeles County/USC Medical Center I worked as a general practitioner then joined the Peace Corps in West Africa. It was very important to me to use my skills in a country that has access to such a small number of doctors. I never had a role model but I have always had a variety of people I looked up to or admired. Perhaps that is why my life has had so many interesting twists and turns.

When I returned to the United States I once again worked as a general

Cracked Wheat Launcher Sandwich

2	slices of cracked wheat bread (toasted if preferred)	3	slices medium tomato
1	teaspoon low calorie mayonnaise (optional)	4	slices peeled avocado alfalfa sprouts
1	large lettuce leaf (Romaine, red leaf or iceberg)		black pepper, salt (optional)

You Will Need
positively 1 adult buddy
bread board
knife

teaspoon
toaster
1   sheet of paper towel

1. Toast 2 slices of bread.
2. Spread toast with mayonnaise (optional).
3. Rinse lettuce leaf under water, pat dry with paper towel and place on slice of bread.
4. Place slices of tomato on top of lettuce leaf.
5. Place avocado slices on top of tomatoes
6. Cover tomatoes with handful of alfalfa sprouts.
7. Place other slice of bread on top of alfalfa sprouts; cut sandwich in half.

Mae C. Jemison

practitioner. I also applied to the National Aeronautics and Space Administration. It was a first step toward becoming an astronaut.

It was a dream come true when the call came from NASA that I had been chosen to be the first black woman to fly in space. Space programs are important to me because they present the opportunity to help all people. And of course, my family members were the first persons I called with the news. Although they were as thrilled as I was with the news they couldn't resist telling me they'd known all the time I'd be chosen. That was just the beginning. A year of study and training followed. My assignments since then have included launch support activities at the Kennedy Space Center in Florida and a seven day cooperative space mission between the United States and Japan focusing on life sciences and materials processing experiments.

Quincy Jones

Use your time to practice — it takes days and weeks and years of practice to arrive at your personal best whether it's music or math or biology. And don't forget to give something back. Imagine what a harmonious world it could be if every single person, both young and old, shared a little of what he is good at doing.

The day that I knew I loved music was my childhood's happiest day because it gave me a focus that has lasted all of my life. From that day on, my favorite subject was music and anything related to it. If you think about it, music is one of the most powerful forces on earth. It can make people laugh and cry, dance, sing, protest, it will float you off to sleep or wake you up and even cause you to fall in love. My love of music grew from playing the trumpet to include instrumentation, composing, writing lyrics, arranging, producing shows, and of course performing. But it didn't happen all at once.

There were eight children in my family, my brother and me and six half and step brothers and sisters. We had lived in the inner city of Chicago, Illinois until I was ten, then we moved to a town near Seattle, Washington because my father, who was a carpenter, got a job in a Navy shipyard during World War II, and wanted us to live in a better environment. That proved to be a fortunate move for me because I got involved in music, both as a singer and as a trumpet player. Although I didn't take trumpet lessons until I was older with Mr. Lewis, my barber, and Clark Terry, who was with Count Basie at the time, I loved

QUINCY
JONES
Composer/Arranger/Producer
Los Angeles, California

to listen to jazz recordings and practiced the trumpet and piano on my own. All that practice helped when I joined The Bumps Blackwell Jr. Band and met Ray Charles. Ray was sixteen and I was fourteen. I continued to sing in vocal groups, sing in church and play in bands as the years passed.

For me, I felt it was important to get formal training so I could continue to grow in my musical career. Although I feel I am a very creative person, the training I received both at Berklee School of Music and as a student of Nadia Boulanger in Paris, France was extremely helpful. It gave me the tools to translate my thoughts and ideas onto paper or musical scores and into words other musicians can understand. In the final analysis, the school of the streets is the real deal, where you have to just *do it*. As an artist, I find it very enjoyable to be surrounded with other artists. That's one of the great things about working as a composer and producer.

After finishing school, I began to think about writing the music that is heard in motion pictures. That was an area that had been mostly closed to blacks, but I refused to change my dreams. I created the music for a film in Sweden and soon was given the opportunity to write the music for American movies.

It's been exciting expressing my own creativity in music, videos, film and in

Medley of Greens

2	pounds collard, mustard or turnip greens (tender with thin stems)	½	teaspoon brown sugar (optional)	
1	teaspoon olive oil	½	cup chicken broth (fat removed) or water	
1	clove garlic (peeled and minced)	1	large white turnip (peeled and diced)	
2	ounces turkey ham (diced)	¼	teaspoon cider vinegar	
½	thinly sliced medium onion			

You Will Need

1	harmonizing grown up assistant	potholder
	large non-stick skillet	can opener
	sharp knife	cutting board
	measuring spoon and cup	large mixing spoon

1. Wash greens thoroughly to remove sand. Cut across into 1-inch pieces.
2. Heat olive oil in skillet over low heat, add garlic and sauté until soft. Add turkey ham and cook 2 minutes.
3. Add greens, onions, brown sugar, chicken broth and diced turnip.
4. Cover pan and turn heat to medium, cook for five minutes until greens wilt. Add vinegar.
5. Gently stir greens. Cover. Lower heat and cook for an additional 15 minutes. (Tougher greens may require a little longer cooking time.)
6. Season to taste, remove from pan and serve.

Serves 6

Quincy Jones

print. Working with people like Clark Terry, Dizzy Gillespie, Duke Ellington, Count Basie and Ray Charles has enriched me beyond words. But along with all the excitement of composing music for *Roots* and producing records for people like Michael Jackson, or a movie like *The Color Purple* there is another part of me that is not satisfied until I give something back. That is why I wanted to produce the *We Are The World* record to benefit the hungry persons of the world and draw attention to them. I think it is so important, no matter what your career, to set aside time to stay connected to your community—to share a little of what you do well to help others.

Family is very important to me, too. My father encouraged me to maximize my talent by practicing my music. I still do. My grandmother was special to me also, and she made the best greens in the world. Perhaps that's why I like soul food better than anything else. It tastes earthier than anything else I've ever eaten. Cooking is my hobby. It gives me the opportunity to make and taste all kinds of delicious foods.

Barbara Jordan

People look at those who have made their mark in the world and forget that the journey began in childhood. Families, teachers, friends, school experiences, even our neighborhoods and towns are influences in our lives. But we can choose our own direction. The important thing is to study choices, decide what is important to you and act on it.

I grew up without television in a segregated area of Houston, Texas never really knowing what might be possible in terms of other lifestyles. My world consisted of our neighborhood, my friends and family. My Grandfather Patten and I were especially close because he showed an interest in me and encouraged me to do my own thinking. He had his own junk business and did as he wanted. After church on Sunday I looked forward to the big dinner we'd eat at his house. I could smell the aroma of pot roast, greens, and peach cobbler as we entered the house.

Grandfather Patten showed me how to weigh out the rags and the fertilizer that folks came to buy. And, he trusted me to handle the money. I was careful with all that money because I didn't want to lose his trust. He paid me for the work I did and that made me feel powerful, like a miniature adult able to buy some of the things that I wanted. Grandfather encouraged me to make my own decisions and take care of myself. I needed that encouragement because I planned for my life to be different. I had

BARBARA
JORDAN
**Law Professor, University at Austin
Austin, Texas**

thoughts of becoming a lawyer, even though I wasn't sure exactly what lawyers did.

School was an interesting time for me. I joined the All Girl's Choir and used my outspoken nature to my advantage on the debate team. I liked challenging my peers and teachers but I also was fortunate to have teachers who took time to boost my confidence. Even though I was smart I needed someone to pick out the things I was good at and remind me of my strengths.

I was always looking at the world, examining it—especially the issues of segregation. It seemed strange and oddly sad that there were black people and white people in the world but that there seemed to be no common ground where the two ever met. I was glad to be able to voice my own views during a debate about segregation. I liked thinking about important issues and arguing them in debates. I did not know then, but debating was training for a lifetime highlight, giving the keynote address for the Democratic National Convention in 1976. But right then my thoughts were on high school and one of my happiest days was when I was chosen "Girl of the Year" at Phyllis Wheatley High School. My whole family came to see me accept the honor.

Later on when I had finished college and law school, I put my public

Honey Peach Cobbler

Preheat oven to 400°.
Bake 25 minutes.

See Broccoli Quiche recipe (page 67) for pie dough, or use a purchased 9-inch refrigerated pie shell
1 28-ounce can sliced peaches, drained (reserve one cup of syrup)
1 teaspoon lemon juice

¼ cup honey
1 teaspoon cornstarch
1 teaspoon flour
½ teaspoon cinnamon
½ teaspoon nutmeg
*1 tablespoon vegetable margarine (melted)
1 beaten egg white

You Will Need
1 adult helper
rolling pin
knife
measuring spoons
measuring cup
pastry brush

large spoon
2-quart saucepan
fork
oven mitts
1-quart baking dish

1. Place peaches and lemon in 1-quart baking dish. Mix and set aside.
2. In 2-quart saucepan combine and mix honey, cornstarch, flour, cinnamon, and nutmeg. Add reserved syrup and margarine.
3. Bring mixture to a boil, stir constantly until thickened; pour over peaches and let cool.
4. Roll 1 pie shell (only) and place on top of peaches. Trim excess dough with knife, then crimp along the edges with fork.
5. Brush beaten egg white on dough; then pierce crust with fork to permit steam to escape during baking.
6. Use oven mitts to remove peach cobbler from oven. Let sit for 25 minutes before serving.

*See note for margarine, page 10.

Serves 6

Barbara Jordan

speaking skills to work to help our local Democrats get elected. Friends suggested I run for public office. I lost my first two elections but I didn't let that stop me. Instead of giving up I took the time to find out why I lost. People asked how many times I was going to run for office when I announced I was a Texas Senate candidate. Once more, I said. When I won, it was the beginning of life in public office. Later I ran for the House of Representatives and won. All because I never gave up.

Jawanza Kunjufu

Never use the word can't. With God,
all things are possible.

I was born and grew up in Chicago, Illinois with one sister who is younger than me. My parents worked hard, but, always had time for us and encouraged us to do well in school. In the sixth grade I had a fantastic teacher, Mrs. Butler. Her rule was that each student should aim for 110 percent. Her expectations were high for us and we worked hard to meet them. It's a funny thing when you realize that someone has great expectations for you; you begin to have great expectations for yourself. Imagine how happy I was when told I was going to skip the seventh grade. All that work made a big difference and caused one of the happiest days of my life.

I continue to apply Mrs. Butler's 110 percent rule to everything I do. After the sixth grade I lived in a single parent home and I stuttered, a problem I worked hard to overcome. All that practice with speaking paid off. Now a part of my work involves standing up before a room full of people and giving speeches.

JAWANZA
KUNJUFU, Ph.D.
Author, Lecturer
Chicago, Illinois

Sometimes students are criticized for being smart. In my book, *To Be Popular or Smart*, I suggest that students should try to be diverse in their interests and excel in other areas besides academics, such as sports, music, or art. It's also important to choose friends who reinforce your value system and to develop strong self-esteem. Parents can help children to feel good about themselves and resist negative peer pressure by building self-esteem. Teaching children to contribute in meaningful ways to the operation of a home helps develop capabilities. It takes a little time and patience to coach children in new activities. To avoid discouragement, choose a time when both you and your child aren't under time pressure and are feeling relaxed. Remember praise in what is learned, not critical remarks, support learning.

The subject I loved best in school was math. I always had this thought even when I was a kid, that I would be my own boss and own my own business. It helps an author and lecturer if he is a self-starter and independent. Good communication skills are very important too. Other work possibilities are newspaper and magazine writing and television broadcasting. It is not too soon to start giving 110 percent. A good writer is a good reader. And, if you have an opportunity to speak, whether in a classroom, or a church, or to any group, don't pass it up.

Speaking and writing are important because they allow me to influence people. I meet new people everyday and have many opportunities to exchange ideas.

Scholarly Broccoli Quiche

Preheat oven to 350°.

1 prepared whole wheat crust in 9-inch deep-dish pie pan (recipe follows)
1½ cups broccoli flowerets (cut into small pieces)
¼ cup finely chopped green onions
2 eggs + 2 egg whites (beaten)

1 cup evaporated skim milk
⅓ cup low-fat ricotta cheese
½ teaspoon salt
¼ teaspoon white pepper
⅛ teaspoon nutmeg
1 cup shredded low fat Swiss cheese

You Will Need

1 food-loving adult
measuring cup and spoons
large bowl
mixing spoon

pot holders
steamer pot with lid
knife
9-inch deep-dish pie pan

1. Place water in steamer (about 1 inch), bring water to a boil, add broccoli, cover, and steam buds until they become a bright green (about 5 minutes) and set aside to cool.
2. In large bowl place beaten eggs, evaporated skim milk, ricotta cheese, salt, pepper and nutmeg. Stir until thoroughly mixed.
3. Layer half of the Swiss cheese and all of the broccoli on the bottom of the pie shell.
4. Pour the egg mixture over the broccoli and sprinkle with remaining Swiss cheese.
5. Bake 45 to 50 minutes until knife inserted near the center comes out clean.

Pie Dough for Broccoli Quiche

½ cup whole wheat pastry flour and ½ cup unbleached all purpose flour, sifted, OR
1 cup unbleached all purpose flour, sifted

¼ teaspoon salt
2 tablespoons non-fat milk or water
⅛ teaspoon sugar
¼ cup vegetable oil

1. Combine flour, salt and sugar in a bowl and stir.
2. In a separate bowl, mix oil and milk together and pour into flour mixture. Stir with fork until mixture begins to come together.
3. Form into a ball, then press with your hands to make a 5-inch circle. Wrap in plastic wrap and refrigerate for ½ hour.
4. On a lightly floured surface, roll out crust to a 10-inch round and carefully fit into a 9-inch pie pan.

Jawanza Kunjufu

No matter what my schedule, my favorite meal at holidays or anytime is Broccoli Quiche. It's great tasting, especially with a whole wheat crust. It's one of those complete meals in a dish and I always enjoy it.

Iris Marie Mack

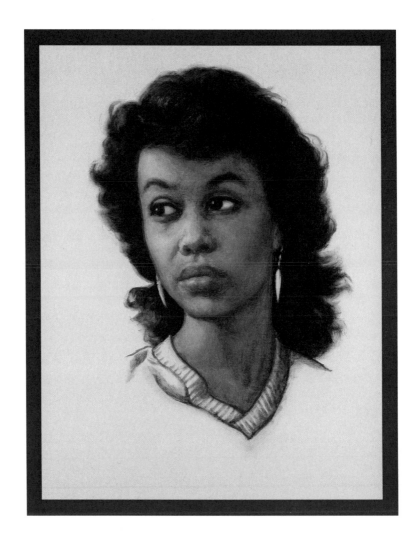

Do what you are best at and what you really think you want to do. Don't let anyone tell you what you should do. But, have a second thing, as an outlet. Be realistic and have something to fall back on. Not many people can become great athletes or musicians. Have a goal and strive to be balanced and flexible, but enjoy the process of getting to that goal.

I was born in New Orleans, Louisiana, the city of river boats, music, Creole food, and the Mardi Gras. There were ten children in our family, each of us competitive in a fun and supportive way. I was a tomboy and still enjoy running and working out with the track club. A favorite sport was playing football in the backyard. I can still hear the crack of my shoulder breaking when one of the older kids tackled me. Once it healed I was back out there again. I also played clarinet in the school band and loved to entertain my parents with musical productions with my brothers and sisters. With such a large family, holidays have always been special at our home with delicious dinners. With all my activities it's no wonder that to this day, my most favorite food is a scrumptious, gigantic, crunchy, vitamin packed salad, topped with toasted sesame seeds or almonds.

My parents were interested in politics, sports, and church activities and kept us involved too. They handled a lot of things without much money but kept a balance, enjoying life along the way. They had one rule we had to follow. We had to get our chores and our homework done first,

IRIS MARIE
MACK, Ph.D.
Consultant, Researcher, Applied Mathematics and Financial Engineering El Sobrante, California

then we could go out. My brothers and sisters and I sometimes felt like we were in the Army because we had a disciplined lifestyle. We even threatened at times to run away. Later, when I went to Vassar College I realized it would have been a disaster without being disciplined and organized. Some Saturdays while my college friends were partying I was doing math problem sets. But it's just like music, you can't get to Tschaikovsky without first paying your dues.

In high school I discovered I liked analytical things. When I got to college I majored in math and physics because I liked them and I was good at them. I knew that college would cost a lot of money and that I'd need to get a scholarship. At summer jobs in high school I saw the different ways employees are treated. That made me determined to do well and get my college degree. Education for me was a practical way to a better life. I thought of it as a luxury. My parents did not have the opportunity that I had and I know what they went through to get us there. The civil rights movement also helped me get to where I was. In fact, I was the second African-American woman to receive a doctorate in Applied Mathematics at Harvard and the first African-American to receive a faculty appointment in the M.I.T. De-

High Power Salad

4 cups mixed salad greens (any kind) spinach, lettuce, red cabbage
½ small zucchini, sliced
1 carrot, peeled and diced
½ cup broccoli flowerets
½ cup cauliflower flowerets, cut small
4 mushrooms, sliced
1 rib celery, sliced
½ red onion, sliced thin

½ cucumber, sliced thin
¼ cup garbanzo beans
½ cup green bell pepper, sliced
1 cup leftover cooked pasta (if desired)
½ cup snow peas (if desired)
2 tablespoons low-calorie salad dressing of your choice
1 tomato, cut into 8 wedges toasted sesame seeds or almonds, to taste

You Will Need
1 salad-loving adult helper
1 large bowl
  sharp knife

cutting board
large spoon
fork

1. Wash, pat dry, and gently tear salad greens to make 4 cups and set aside.
2. Place all other vegetables and pasta in the bowl. Set tomato wedges aside for later use.
3. Toss vegetables with 2 tablespoons of your favorite low-calorie dressing.
4. Gently fold in 4 cups of salad greens.
5. Garnish top of salad with tomato wedges.
6. Sprinkle toasted sesame seeds and/or almonds on top.

Serves 4

Iris Marie Mack

partment of Applied Mathematics. Someone paid for my opportunity and I was determined to do my best.

I still love music, it's one of my hobbies. As for sports, you name it, I love it; body building, weight lifting, hiking, aerobics, dancing, water games, yoga, flying and track. I run five days a week and new ideas, like my "The Olympics of Thinkers" (TOOT) program, come to me while I'm jogging. I want to implement TOOT to prepare mental athletes for international intellectual competitions similar to our sports Olympics. I know the type of training mathematicians, scientists and engineers undergo to excel. Without mathematicians the world would lack the excitement of a blast off into space, cars, skyscrapers, and computers. Math creates wonderful careers. Because of my background I was chosen to spend two months in the middle of the Atlantic Ocean on a research vessel using math to study wave motion.

Leatrice B. McKissack

Ninety-five percent of life is an attitude thing. Enjoy every moment; the fresh smell of cut grass, a walk in the woods, in other words enjoy every second of your life. Take good care of yourself and never worry about anything. Put it in God's hands and trust in him.

I was fortunate in my childhood that I was the second child with three younger brothers. My mother never made any difference between me and my brothers, we all were expected to do the same jobs. During family gatherings the children would play together while my grandmother, mother and aunts did the cooking. It made me feel like an important part of the family when I was allowed to help prepare the food and to share in the conversation.

Those days were filled with the warmth and closeness of family and relatives. My parents often shared with the children stories of what had happened in their lives. As an adult, I have carried on the tradition of family gatherings. Spending quality time with my children and godchildren has always been a priority. Now my daughters and I can't wait to get together. We take retreats together with a "hotseat" tradition. We ask each person, "Now what's going on in your life that you're not happy about?" then we bounce ideas off one another. That time of sharing and involving family members in our lives keeps our family strong and connected.

LEATRICE
McKISSACK
CEO, McKissack & McKissack, Architects and Engineers Nashville, Tennessee

My childhood dream of becoming a teacher did come true but after 17 years I retired for my health. I don't have time for negativism. I believe if you're not smiling you ought to be. And so, I took my parent's lead. They set an example of voluntarism which I followed and I took up flower gardening. I am a gourmet cook and each Monday evening I held dinner parties for my husband's clients. Later, when I suddenly inherited the architectural firm of McKissack & McKissack those same clients stood by me. The firm is the oldest black architectural firm in the country and I wanted to try to keep it in the family even though I had no architectural background. I spent a lot of time reading to learn what was going on in the company, and searching through files. My oldest daughter resigned her job and came home to help me. I believe when you throw out a boomerang — it always comes back to you one way or another. Along with those clients staying with me, the skills I learned with flower gardening enabled me to do the landscape architecture on an important project.

The hardest part of my career today is keeping up with my schedule. Because I am the chief executive officer of McKissack & McKissack I am involved or on numerous committees, commissions, and boards. My work

Enchanted Fried Corn

6	ears of fresh corn		1	teaspoon sugar
1	green onion (sliced across, green part only)		½	teaspoon salt
			½	cup water
¼	cup red bell pepper (diced)		*2	tablespoons vegetable margarine
1	tablespoon flour			

You Will Need

1	adult assistant		wide metal spatula
1	sharp paring knife		large mixing spoon
1	bowl		measuring cup
1	large skillet		measuring spoon

1. Husk corn, remove all silk and wash.
2. Score corn vertically through the center of each row of kernels. (The secret of this recipe is by cutting down through the center of the kernels, the corn-milk is released.)
3. Cut corn from the cob into bowl; then scrape all remaining liquid and pulp from cob into the bowl.
4. Add onion, peppers, flour, sugar, salt, water and stir.
5. Heat margarine in skillet on high heat. Carefully pour corn mixture into hot skillet. Cook mixture until it begins to form crust on the bottom.
6. Now reduce the heat to low. Cook the corn mixture for 10 minutes until corn kernels are done.
7. Spoon top of corn mixture into a serving dish. Use spatula to lift the browned corn crust from bottom of skillet, then carefully place on top of corn and serve at once.

*See margarine note, page 10.

Serves 4

Leatrice B. McKissack

appeals to me because it's creative. Architects plan and design buildings, working with people to develop the kinds of structures that meet their needs. Along with the National Civil Rights Museum in Memphis, Tennessee, our firm designs hospitals, commercial and religious buildings and is on ten college campuses.

If you practice the Golden Rule, *"Do unto others as you would have them do unto you,"* life will be most rewarding. I have always felt that spending quality time with children is so important. And, I still enjoy cooking. Fresh fried corn is my favorite recipe because my mother-in-law, Miranda McKissack, taught me how to prepare it. I think it is the best fried corn recipe in the world.

Evelyn K. Moore

*Children are our most precious resource.
To work to develop national programs and
policies affecting the future of children is a
natural extension of my love and concern
for the welfare of all children.*

I was born in the city of Detroit, Michigan into a very large family, six girls and three boys. My dad was a great organizer, he had to be with so many children. There was a real sense of excitement whenever he announced that we were going on a picnic. He'd send one of us for the tablecloths, another for the sports equipment, someone else for the picnic basket. You can imagine the flurry of activity in our home as nearly a dozen people tried to get ready to go somewhere. Besides picnics, one of my fondest remembrances of my childhood are the home baked foods my mother made, especially the hot rolls. Their aroma would fill the house.

I've always enjoyed sports. The challenge, technique and coordination necessary for tennis has always had the greatest appeal for me. That's why I love it, whether I'm a spectator or participant.

One of the places that I couldn't wait to go when I was a child was school. My first grade teacher, Johnnie Scott, was the person who most inspired me. She was the one who taught me how

EVELYN
MOORE
Executive Director
National Black Child Development Institute
Washington, D.C.

to read, and it has been a life-long hobby for me. Thanks to Mrs. Scott, I grew up wanting to be a teacher. I have always thought that children were very special. That is why I went to college and got a degree in special education along with a master's degree in education.

My interest in the welfare of children has led me down several paths. I frequently write and speak about issues related to children and teens such as day care, adoption, foster care, health, and education. I've found that one informed, enthusiastic person can make a difference, and I am committed to doing just that. That is why I started the National Black Child Development Institute. It is a place where I can work with my staff to raise funds for programs for the most important people in the world—children. It is located in Washington, D.C., our nation's capital, so it is in a good location for us to promote programs that help children and families.

Coming from a big family, I cherish the times spent around the family table where we would talk out our problems, share our dreams of the future and discuss our daily activities. We also spent time together planting tomatoes and corn in the family garden and pulling up weeds on warm summer days. Of course, we were expected to string the beans and peel the apples and set

Tangy Chicken Breast

	vegetable non-stick spray	2	teaspoons honey	
4	chicken breast halves	1	teaspoon soy sauce	
1	teaspoon olive oil	⅛	teaspoon pepper	
1	clove garlic (crushed)	1	tablespoon chili sauce	
2	teaspoons balsamic vinegar		or catsup	

You Will Need

1	adult partner		broiler pan with rack
1	large bowl		paper towels
	long-handled fork		measuring spoons
	long-handled spoon		knife
2	oven mitts		

1. Spray broiler pan and rack with non-stick spray.
2. Wash chicken breasts and pat dry with paper towels.
3. Mix olive oil, garlic, vinegar, honey, soy sauce, pepper and chili sauce in bowl to make marinade.
4. Add chicken breasts (skin side down) and marinate for 10 minutes.
5. Place marinated chicken breasts onto rack-pan (skin side up). Broil for 7 minutes; then turn chicken over; spoon remaining marinade over chicken and broil for another 7 minutes.
6. Pierce meatiest part of chicken with fork. If juice runs clear, it is cooked. If juice is still pink, cook a little longer until it is done.
7. Turn oven off.
8. Use mitts to carefully remove pan from oven.

Serves 4

Evelyn K. Moore

the table too. But that was okay with me. It just meant it would be that much quicker for dinner to be served, which included my favorites, grilled chicken, fresh corn on the cob, sliced tomatoes and deep dish apple pie.

Alvin F. Poussaint

It's important to develop individually but it's also important and strengthening to reach out and help other people. Try to do your best, admitting your deficiencies if you have any, knowing that if you work at them you can correct them. Some self-doubt is normal but never start anything with an attitude of total self-doubt.

I was born in New York City into a family of eight children. At the age of nine my parents took me to the hospital where they discovered I had rheumatic fever. I was there for six months. The hospital was strict about visitors and my family visited me once each week. Alone and isolated, I turned to books and the hospital staff to help pass the lonely hours and began to think about becoming a doctor myself. Getting sick seemed like a stumbling block to me, but it was actually a stepping stone. All that reading helped me be more effective academically and I began to see in books a little of what life had to offer outside of my neighborhood.

Nothing in my background would have steered me towards becoming a doctor although I was naturally good at science. I had a brother who was always in trouble. My mother died when I was in junior high school and I lived in a pretty rough neighborhood. A lot of my friends were strung out on heroin. Kids were dying of drug overdoses or being killed. I had a lot of chores to do at home. Somtimes finding enough hours to do my school work was difficult. Instead of defeating me it made me determined to do something with myself to escape. I had seen a little of the other side of life while I was in the hospital and I clung to my dream of becoming a doctor.

ALVIN F. POUSSAINT, M.D.
Psychiatrist
Boston, Massachusetts

All the while, my family supported me in my dream although they may not have thought it could be a reality. My friends used to call me "The Brain" in a teasing but nice way, giving me confidence that I was smart. My sister-in-law, Bobbi Poussaint, inspired me while I was in junior high school by taking an interest in my schoolwork. She attended a school of social work and gave me her books to read, then discussed them with me. A lot of my support for school and career goals came from teachers and community centers.

Being a psychiatrist allows me to influence good mental health practices by helping people understand and overcome things that interfere with their growth as a person. I can work to eliminate racism and discrimination through my writing. I can be an educator and a teacher. Both my race and socio-economic background help me tune into issues in my clients' lives. When I say, don't let anyone's attitudes and biases defeat you, clients recognize their struggles may be similar to my own. I tell them, you must struggle to accomplish what you want to accomplish and not retreat. Don't

Savory Boiled Ribs and Cabbage

2	pounds spare ribs (small end)	½	small bay leaf
1	small onion, chopped	2	pounds cabbage, cut in eighths
2	cloves garlic, minced		
1	1-inch slice of bell pepper, diced		Seasoning mix
		½	teaspoon paprika
1	3-inch rib of celery, sliced	¼	teaspoon black pepper
3	cups water, divided	¼	teaspoon oregano leaves
		¼	teaspoon garlic salt

You Will Need

1	adult assistant		small paring knife
	large non-stick skillet with cover	1	large fork
			small bowl
	measuring cup		pot holder
	sharp cutting knife		

1. Wash ribs, pat dry, cut into six sections; remove all fat, then rub rib sections with seasoning mix.
2. Heat non-stick skillet over high heat. Place ribs in skillet and brown on all sides (about 5 minutes).
3. Remove ribs from skillet and lower heat to medium; add onion, garlic, bell pepper, celery and ¼ cup water; stir until vegetables are tender.
4. Return ribs to skillet with vegetables. Add bay leaf and remaining 2¾ cups water (or enough water to cover). Put lid on skillet, and cook for about 45 minutes or until nearly done.
5. Remove ribs; cool; scrape off any remaining fat.
6. Pour liquid from skillet into a bowl; skim any fat which comes to the surface.
7. Return ribs and liquid to skillet; place cabbage on top of ribs; bring to a boil, cover, lower heat, cook until cabbage is done (about 15 minutes). Season to taste.

Serves 6

Alvin F. Poussaint

let others damage your self-esteem. Talk with each other and with parents for mutual support. During the 1960's I was able to be political in the civil rights movement and spent two years in Mississippi. Later, my background allowed me to become director of student affairs at Harvard Medical School.

With all that's happened in my life, I still remember that day my parents took me home from the hospital after my six month stay. It was wonderful being with my family, and I could hardly wait to taste my mom's boiled ribs and cabbage.

Julius S. Scott, Jr.

*People who have changed history have been
those committed to values and goals,
who have a sense of destiny, and who
are willing to seek the welfare of others
before their own.*

The embracing warmth of the family gave everyone a sense of caring and belonging when I was a child. Sunday dinner was my favorite meal of the week, because it was a time for family gathering and conversations. Once in a while there would be house guests and friends staying for dinner, which would add to the variety of topics we discussed. On holidays mother's stewed okra with tomatoes, black eyed peas and potato pies were favorites along with turkey and dressing, boiled onions and sweet potatoes topped off with lemon pie and lemonade. My role when the meal was finished was to clean the dishes. I liked drying dishes rather than washing them. I liked to tell jokes and listen to my father, who told good and interesting stories. I also liked to share what was happening with me. It was fun to talk about my hobbies; photography and stamp collecting.

JULIUS S.
SCOTT, JR., Ph.D.
President, Paine College
Augusta, Georgia

Seeing my father in the role of college president was a source of pride and inspiration for me. I loved to go to his office and sit behind his seemingly huge desk and look out over the college campus. It wasn't hard for me to imagine myself as a college president. But I felt that since there were so few presidents, it would be difficult for me to follow in his path. However, I was encouraged to be a leader by my teachers in college and by my colleagues.

I was denied access to some educational opportunities but I didn't let that stop me. Most people have difficulties in their lives and they can choose a way around them or give up. I decided what I wanted out of life was worth struggling for. I was taught by competent and inspiring persons who helped me to understand that I could achieve whatever I wanted. I think we can learn from both the good and bad that happens in our lives and even use it to our advantage. This sense of struggling against the odds was excellent preparation for my role as a college president.

Reading is the best preparation for intellectual and administrative leadership. One must also speak English well and effectively, and develop early the desire to be the best possible student and person you are capable of being. Teaching is an excellent preparation for the college presidency, as is professional involvement and being a leader of a group. The ability to lead is the primary prerequisite for a college presidency. In addition, one must have an engaging personality, a sense of values and direction, the ability to make wise decisions and stick by them, and the ability to raise funds and make

A Stupendous Stew For You
~with Okra, Tomatoes and Corn

1	medium onion, chopped	1	7 ounce can whole kernel corn, drained	
½	small bell pepper, chopped			
1	teaspoon olive oil	½	teaspoon dried basil	
½	pound okra (small) washed, pod removed and sliced ½-inch across	¼	teaspoon dried oregano	
		½	teaspoon sugar (optional) salt and pepper to taste (optional)	
1	15 ounce can whole, peeled tomatoes, coarsely chopped			

You Will Need

	a vegetable loving grown up helper	1	cutting knife
	non-stick skillet		measuring spoons
		1	large wooden spoon

1. Sauté chopped onion and bell pepper with olive oil in skillet over low heat until soft.
2. Add okra, raise heat to medium and cook for 5 minutes, stirring occasionally with wooden spoon.
3. Add tomatoes, corn, basil, oregano, sugar and stir to mix well.
4. Lower heat and cook an additional 10 minutes.
5. Serve at once.

Serves 6

 Julius S. Scott, Jr.

friends. The most time-consuming and difficult part of the responsibility is raising adequate funds. This requires constant attention, planning, and activity.

The travel involved in my work as college president is exciting, as is meeting a variety of people from all walks of life. The challenges include providing the vision and managing the resources of the college. Happiness and fulfillment come from seeing students who succeed. My own personal philosophy for success in life and career is to have a sense of humor, treat people with dignity and respect, be confident, and have a set of standards and beliefs which make a difference in your life.

Calvin J. Stewart, Jr.

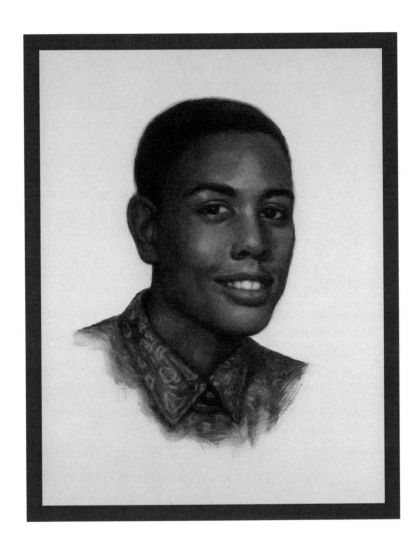

*If I could take just one piece of knowledge
with me and journey back through
my childhood I would take to heart
Philippians 4:13 — I can do all things
through Christ who strengthens me.*

I was born in Hattiesburg, Mississippi. I have one brother and we were best pals. We played games and participated in sports, although I was diagnosed with sickle cell anemia at age four. I tire easily, so I make certain to get plenty of rest. No matter what, I keep a positive attitude; it helps me conquer many things. I pray, exercise to keep fit, take my medicine, eat a diet high in fruits and vegetables—and get on with my life.

At home, ground beef, bell peppers, onions, and seasonings meant my favorite meatloaf for supper. To hurry up the process, I'd ask Mom if she needed any help, and she'd put me to work scraping carrots while we talked. The aroma of my mother's meatloaf is indescribable. And, once you've smelled it, you would know it and wouldn't forget it for a long time.

As happy as those memories are, there were sad and difficult times for my mother, my brother, and myself when we moved to Washington, D.C. There was no affordable housing for a single parent with two children. We lived in a shelter for people without a home. My mother and Jesus became my biggest inspirations, they were always there for me. I needed that because I didn't fit in with some of the gangs and

**CALVIN J.
STEWART, JR.**

**College Student, Eastern
Connecticut University
Willimantic, Connecticut**

rough kids. And, I didn't have many friends. My mother helped me get through the problems of living in a terrible environment, "Never lose hope," she'd say. I saw what could happen to people who were less goal-oriented and it made me more determined to work hard in school and to better myself.

At the shelter, a professional photographer befriended us kids by teaching us photography. It was important to us that others didn't tease us or pity us. We wanted to be treated like anyone else. I soon discovered I loved photography. It allowed me to express a part of me that most people don't know exists. People are my favorite subjects because they are unpredictable and distinct artistic patterns. One of my most thrilling days was when I opened up the October 8, 1991 issue of *U.S. News and World Report.* My first published photograph, a picture of my friend Fred hanging on the lightpost, was there for everyone to see. I called to share the news with my mother, then my father. They were excited and very proud. The next month my photograph of two children walking down the steps of Malcolm X Park holding hands was published in *Life* magazine.

Picture Perfect Meat Loaf

Preheated 350° oven.

4	egg whites or 2 eggs
2	pounds ground turkey
½	cup canned tomato sauce
1½	cups whole wheat bread crumbs (about 4 slices grated)
¼	cup plain yogurt
⅓	cup red bell peppers, diced in ¼ inch pieces
¼	cup green onions, chopped
¼	cup fresh parsley, chopped fine

2	cloves garlic, minced
2	teaspoons dried Italian herbs
½	teaspoon black pepper
1	tablespoon lemon juice
½	teaspoon salt
	paprika
	a few parsley sprigs and cherry tomato halves may be used for garnish

You Will Need

1	hungry adult helper
1	large mixing bowl
	fork
1	grater
	measuring cups
	measuring spoons
	large mixing spoon

	knife
1	9x5x3-inch loaf pan
	non-stick vegetable spray
	potholders
1	serving platter
	spatula

1. Spray loaf pan with vegetable spray and set aside.
2. Place egg whites in bowl and beat slightly with fork.
3. Place all ingredients except paprika, parsley sprigs, and cherry tomatoes into the bowl with egg whites.
4. Stir ingredients with spoon until well mixed.
5. Place mixture into greased loaf pan and pat into loaf shape.
6. Sprinkle top of meat loaf with paprika.
7. Place pan in preheated oven and bake for 60 minutes.
8. Turn off oven, cool for 10 minutes. Remove loaf from pan using spatula and place on platter; garnish with parsley sprigs and sliced cherry tomato halves.

Serves 8

Calvin J. Stewart, Jr.

Through photography I won a college scholarship. I realized my freshman year at college that high school and college are much different. It took much more studying than I expected. But, I also found that accomplishments and rewards gained are far greater and more important than the time spent struggling to achieve them.

Debi Thomas

Don't listen when people discourage you from trying to achieve according to your own plans and needs. Combining school and skating and fun felt right to me, and so I did it — and it worked. By remaining in school— even if I lost skating competitions — I still came out a winner.

When I was a little girl in kindergarten my family went to see an ice show. There and then I knew that I would become a figure skater. One of the happiest days of my childhood was when all those hours of practicing finally paid off, and I won my first figure skating competition. I like skating because it is a beautiful sport and it's challenging. But there is a lot more going on behind the scenes than I realized at first.

The outfits figure skaters wear are gorgeous, but very expensive. So are the lessons, which often last six hours a day. I needed to do my part, so I learned to sew my costumes and add each bead. My mom was always encouraging, reminding me that I really could do whatever I wanted to do. She helped me keep a balance as I climbed the figure skating ladder. While I was having a lot of success at skating, there were times that I blew it and lost. When I was thirteen I thought that I couldn't be beat. I was able to do three triple jumps when other skaters couldn't. By losing a big competition that year I ended up winning because I realized there had to be more in my life than skating.

DEBI
THOMAS
Professional Figure Skater
El Granada, California

From the time I could remember going to school, no matter what the subject was, I was always fascinated by the challenge of learning. I wanted to be a doctor and I planned to go to college. I had to figure out a way to go to school and skate at the same time because I didn't want to be in college forever. Sometimes I had to let up on my skating practice schedule so I could concentrate on my classes. Along with all the time at the rink, I had to lift weights and study. I also tried to find time to relax playing golf, or eat a leisurely holiday meal of special foods—turkey with stuffing, corn, and peach pie.

Some people told me I couldn't do it but I didn't listen to them. My mom continued to tell me, "You can do it any way that you want." And so I do. I believe in having fun along with the work of college and skating. That's what feels right for me. Yes, I was a World Figure Skating Champion, and the Bronze Medalist at the 1988 Olympics. But by remaining in school and planning for a future in medicine, I always felt that even if I lost, I was still someone with a future.

My future now is medicine but I've learned lots in skating that I'll never forget. Like how to eat foods for energy. Vegetarian pizza is my all-time favorite food because it's easy and complete. Skating requires tremendous

The Vegetarian Pizza

Preheat oven to 450°.
Bake 20 minutes.

1	16-inch pizza crust	1	teaspoon dried basil
1	yellow crookneck squash, sliced	½	teaspoon Italian seasoning, dried
1	small zucchini, sliced		
1	tablespoon olive oil	½	cup black olives, drained and halved
2	cloves garlic, minced		
2	medium onions, sliced thin	2	tomatoes, sliced
½	red bell pepper, sliced	8	ounces low-fat Mozzarella cheese, grated
½	green bell pepper, sliced		
8	medium mushrooms, sliced		

You Will Need

1	pizza-loving adult helper	1	large spoon
1	steamer pan with cover		cutting knife
1	large non-stick skillet	1	16-inch pizza pan
	measuring spoons and cups	2	potholders

1. Place water in steamer about 1 inch, bring water to a boil, add squash and zucchini and cook for four minutes until color turns bright. Remove immediately.
2. In large skillet, heat oil over medium heat.
3. Put garlic and onions in skillet and cook until transparent.
4. Add sliced peppers, mushrooms, and steamed vegetables over high heat and sauté for about 3 minutes.
5. Add seasonings, olives and stir for an additional 1 minute. Remove from pan and cool slightly.
6. Spread vegetables on prepared pizza crust, cover with sliced tomatoes and drizzle mozzarella cheese throughout.
7. Bake for 20 minutes or until light golden in color.
8. Turn off oven and remove pizza carefully using potholders.

Serves 8

 Debi Thomas

amounts of energy and it was not unusual for my mom to take me to get my favorite food at four o'clock in the morning on the way to skating practice.

Robert Townsend

*It's those who attach their dreams to actions
and let them fly that are the true stars of
this world.*

I've always been an entertainer. My first audiences were the kids on the basketball court in my old neighborhood (on the west side of Chicago). We would be playing ball and I couldn't resist dragging out my impressions to make them laugh. Basketball and impressions were my life, and I practiced both whenever I could.

At home, I would stand in front of the bathroom mirror pretending to be James Earl Jones or Bill Cosby. My mom would pass by and hear strange voices from behind the bathroom door. Her laughter was all the approval I needed. My "career" really began when I entered and won my fifth grade speech contest. The experience of standing alone in front of a large group of people and sharing my thoughts was the greatest feeling.

ROBERT TOWNSEND
Actor/Director/Writer
Los Angeles, California

While I was in college, I commuted to acting lessons with The Negro Ensemble Company in New York. Finding work as an actor was difficult. Not only were few roles available to me as an actor, but the images portrayed made me angry. Black talent was being wasted on limited characters. I wanted to have a turn at being the leading man, but the opportunity wasn't there. I felt that the only way to give myself and other black talent the opportunity they deserved was to create the characters and direct my own projects.

Hollywood Shuffle, my first movie, held up a mirror to the film industry about the way black talent is used and/or abused — that was an important message to me. So to pay for it, I used the only thing I easily had readily available—credit cards. The financial risk was well worth the opportunity to correct the stereotypical images of black people on the screen. The thrill of making a positive impact with my film was beyond comparison. *Hollywood Shuffle* was an immediate success.

In preparation for my second film, *The Five Heartbeats*, I went on the road with a vocal group that had been around since the sixties. I needed to hear and experience firsthand what things had been like. I always want my movies to ring true. I also want to be able to look back on a project and say that what I did was good.

I owe all of my success to my mom. She was always there telling me there was nothing that I couldn't do. It's important to have someone who believes in you, and who you know is in your corner rooting for you. My mom is someone who is proud of me no matter what I do. She's been in my corner since I came into this world. When I was young, I thought the best part of

The Glorious Bird

Preheat oven to 325°.
Bake 3 hours and 30 minutes.

1	14 pound turkey, fresh or defrosted seasoning mix	1	apple, washed and cored
1	large onion, halved	2	tablespoons chicken broth
2	stalks celery, cut in 2-inch pieces	1	tablespoon oil
		¼	teaspoon garlic powder
		¼	teaspoon sage
		½	teaspoon paprika

Seasoning Mix
Combine:

½	teaspoon poultry seasoning	¼	teaspoon pepper
½	teaspoon salt	1	clove garlic, finely minced

You Will Need

1	able-bodied adult	1	meat thermometer
1	turkey roasting pan with lid		poultry skewers
1	turkey baster		small bowl
1	cutting knife		measuring spoons
2	potholders		

1. Remove giblets, neck and trim all visible fat from turkey. Wash turkey thoroughly and pat dry.
2. Rub cavity with seasoning mix and put ½ of the onion and ½ of the celery inside.
3. Place cored apple into neck cavity.
4. Close cavity with skewers; tuck legs inside lower flap of skin; tuck wings under back of turkey and fold neck skin back and attach with skewer.
5. Mix chicken broth, olive oil, garlic powder, sage, paprika in small bowl, the rub mixture on entire surface of the turkey.
6. Place bird on rack in pan; add 1 cup water to pan, remaining onion and celery and cover. Baste every half hour and roast about 3½ hours, remove cover last hour of roasting and baste frequently to produce rich brown color. Turkey is done when thermometer inserted in thigh registers 180°. Remove from oven and let turkey rest for 30 minutes before slicing.

Serves 6 to 10

Robert Townsend

having a mom like mine was the way she cooked. There was nothing better than being outside shooting baskets with the guys on Thanksgiving while my mom and grandmother made dinner. Thanksgiving is my favorite holiday because you get a little of all the foods that I like; turkey, dressing, broccoli, corn bread, sweet potato pie and eggnog.

Rita Walters

*Work hard, set goals and do not be deterred
in life from reaching your goals nor rest
when those goals are met. Continue to climb
and remember to make a contribution to
your community. We do not achieve in a
vacuum, we are strengthened by role models
who have gone before. I see my struggle as
part of a continuum. We stand on other
shoulders and we must offer our shoulders
to those who come after.*

My mother inspired me to "be somebody". She was an excellent cook much like her mother and taught us an appreciation of well prepared food, the mixing of flavors. While she taught me to cook we talked—she was always extremely encouraging. She helped us to understand that we were capable and that there were honorable ways in which to accomplish our goals.

While I have lots of wonderful childhood memories, one that is most prominent is of a summer evening in Kansas. The days were scorching hot and no one had wanted to cook for several days. The weather made even falling asleep difficult. Late one night, we were all sitting on the front porch, my mother, my sisters and me. As we tried to get cooler, the conversation turned to food. Even though it was the middle of the night, we decided to prepare an entire meal. Pickled beets was a part of that meal and that special memory.

RITA DOLORES
WALTERS
Councilwoman
Los Angeles, California

I grew up in Kansas City, Kansas and attended segregated schools. I was fortunate to have teachers, parents and family members who prepared me for the larger world. "Do not let yourself be defined by the world at large," they told me. We understood that being black was not a handicap. I learned to take advantage of all opportunities and to make way for new opportunities.

Childhood was an exciting time for me. My uncle had a working farm in rural Kansas with pigs, cows, two or three horses, and chickens. There were also some animals and fowl that were not a part of the planned constituency of the farm, like snakes, rabbits, quail, and pheasant that helped control the rodents but also bothered the crops. In season some became a part of our meal. I was an adult before I knew quail and pheasant were delicacies.

As a fourth grader I wanted to please my mother. She wanted me to be a teacher of romance languages. I did become a teacher and taught adults in the Los Angeles Unified School District. I value all children and their abilities and that is why I introduced a "no pass/no play" motion as a member of the Los Angeles Board of Education. I was disturbed by the stories I was reading in the newspapers about the hard times of certain athletes who couldn't meet academic standards for colleges. It was heartbreaking to hear of students on athletic scholarships who were injured and lost their scholarships. There were very few school systems that had any standards or grade requirements for students wishing to participate in any extracurricular activity.

Midsummer Night's Pickled Beets

| 1 | pound beets | ½ | cup water |
| ½ | cup vinegar | 1 | tablespoon pickling spice |

You Will Need
1	grownup helper		measuring spoon
2	pots with lids	1	colander
	measuring cup		

1. Cut off the beet greens, leaving 1-inch stem*. Do not remove root at bottom of beet. Wash beets thoroughly.
2. Place beets in a pot and cover with water. Bring to a medium boil and cook for 30-40 minutes or until they are tender.
3. Drain beets in colander then run cold water over them for a few minutes to cool.
4. Put vinegar, water and pickling spice in pot. Slice cooked beets and put in the pot.
5. Bring to a boil and simmer 20 minutes. Chill or eat at room temperature.

*Beet greens may be set aside and steamed separately for a side dish.

Serves 4

Rita Walters

As a member of the second largest school district in the nation I thought, "I can't sit here without changing that." I offered a motion to require a minimum "C" average in every subject at school. That was modified, but the important thing was to help students find a balance in their lives between academics, athletics, clubs, and other extracurricular activities. I did it for the kids and for their futures and they seemed to understand that. Student body officers at all 49 high schools in the Los Angeles City School district voted to support that motion.

After it had been in effect awhile, the mother of one student told me, "I have you to thank for my son going to college with a scholarship. Before the 'no pass/no play' rule, all he thought about was basketball. But he had to study after your rule went into effect. Now he'll have a future."

BASIC SUBSTITUTIONS

If recipe calls for: **You may use:**

Spices

If recipe calls for:	You may use:
1 tablespoon fresh herbs _____	1 teaspoon dried herbs
1 clove garlic, minced _____	¼ teaspoon garlic powder
1 teaspoon dry mustard _____	2 teaspoons prepared mustard
1 teaspoon fresh ginger _____	¼ teaspoon ground ginger
1 teaspoon Italian seasoning _____	¼ teaspoon each of oregano, basil, thyme, rosemary

Flour and Starches

2¾ cups cake flour _____	2½ cups all-purpose
1 tablespoon cornstarch_____	2 tablespoons flour
1 cup self-rising flour _____	1½ teaspoons baking powder, ½ teaspoon salt and all-purpose flour to make 1 cup

Leavening Agent

1 teaspoon baking powder_____	½ teaspoon cream of tartar plus ¼ teaspoon baking soda

Vegetables and Fruits

1 pound fresh mushrooms _____	6 ounces canned mushrooms
1 cup tomato juice _____	½ cup tomato sauce plus ½ cup water
cooked pumpkin _____	cooked squash
1 cup raisins _____	1 cup cut up dates or currants

Dairy Products

1 cup whole milk (fresh) _____	½ cup evaporated milk plus ½ cup water OR non-fat dry milk and water to make 1 cup
1 cup buttermilk _____	1 tablespoon lemon juice plus whole milk to make 1 cup, let stand 5 minutes
1 egg yolk _____	2 egg whites, refrigerated
whole egg _____	egg substitutes

Miscellaneous

1 cup chicken broth _____	1 bouillon cube plus one cup water

Dear Parents:

Some of the most successful reading and math experiences I had with children in the classroom setting was with the use of cooking projects. Each child had his own recipe scrapbook. Great fun was had when the children made pictures of vegetables that talked, rising agents such as yeast, baking powder or baking soda that flew, etc. Pizza advertisements cut and pasted into scrapbooks are an easy way to understand fractions. Reading is natural in cooking, and new words can be written on shopping lists to familiarize children with spelling. But one of the true joys of cooking projects is just being together, sharing an experience, and talking.

Cooking together successfully takes understanding and effort. I know, I've spent years working with both children and adults in the kitchen. The results are well worth the effort. Here are a few tips that will get your project off to a good start.

1. Set aside a time to cook or bake with your older child when you will be relatively free of distractions from the younger children.

2. Remember, in cooking and baking, creativity comes in many forms and styles. Be open to the child's designs and decorating and praise the effort.

3. Capitalize on your child's creativity and interest. If the child chooses a complicated recipe, break it down into steps. Read the recipe and determine what can be done in advance, pre-preparation the night before allows time for a more complex recipe. Here are some tasks that can usually be done ahead of time: prepare vegetables and refrigerate, measure dry ingredients, assemble baking pans and utensils.

Cooking is for everyone. Fathers and daughters, grandfathers and grandsons, aunties and friends. But it's only fun when there is a genuine camaraderie while mixing, measuring, and stirring. So let your youngster take the lead — the key to success is to allow children to experience the whole process on their level, with your love, guidance, and assistance always present.

Thelma Williams